Sustainable Luxury and Social Entrepreneurship

Stories from the Pioneers

SUSTAINABLE
LUXURY
AND **SOCIAL**
ENTREPRENEURSHIP
STORIES FROM THE PIONEERS

**Miguel Angel Gardetti
and María Eugenia Girón**

Greenleaf
PUBLISHING

© 2014 Greenleaf Publishing Limited

Published by Greenleaf Publishing Limited
Aizlewood's Mill
Nursery Street
Sheffield S3 8GG
UK
www.greenleaf-publishing.com

Cover by LaliAbril.com
Printed in the UK on environmentally friendly, acid-free paper
from managed forests by CPI Group (UK) Ltd, Croydon

British Library Cataloguing in Publication Data:
    A catalogue record for this book is available from the British Library.

ISBN-13: 978-1-78353-063-2 [paperback]
ISBN-13: 978-1-78353-149-3 [hardback]
ISBN-13: 978-1-78353-064-9 [PDF ebook]
ISBN-13: 978-1-78353-150-9 [ePub ebook]

This book is dedicated to the future: our children Macarena, Guadalupe, Jaime, Juan and Rodrigo.

Contents

Foreword

Oskar Metsavaht

I've always known I would be an entrepreneur. Even while studying medicine, I'd already felt the need to break the barriers that, often artificially imposed, limit the field of medical practice. This seed of restlessness, which by the way I think is positive, was planted at home, by witnessing the efforts and commitment of my father, a renowned physician, in creating and developing innovative health services in the city he chose to live in.

So, in a way, adventuring into correlated fields of medicine was, to me, a natural path. By starting to design and manufacture comfortable and adequate clothes for my mountain climbing, I've allied scientific knowledge to intuition, creativity and above all enthusiasm. Without harmony between these elements nothing that I've done—and do— would be possible.

To be successful in any endeavour, we must not establish false dichotomies, opposing, for instance, rationality to passion. We must respect and balance these different kinds of knowledge and, according to the circumstances, dose each one in the equation that makes our dreams possible. It's not about favouring one over the other, but rather knowing the right moment to stress and to focus on the aspects that, at that moment, are decisive and complementary. And to believe in our ability to make it happen. To have confidence in ourselves, in our judgement to know the exact moment when these or those specific abilities must be put into practice, and also in our ability to be sensitive—and to sensitise—the reality around us.

To me, there's no way to be a successful businessperson if achievement and accomplishment are not guided by a desire to make a difference in our society. Each day it becomes clearer that we don't have any option other than to seek innovative solutions so that human life may still have a place on our planet. I can no longer see a possible development other than one in which sustainability permeates everything. It is this perception and understanding that make me become committed to the good environmental and social practices I do in the different initiatives I undertake. I have incorporated this engagement—as I have done when I went beyond the field of medicine—very naturally and atavistically. Otherwise, it wouldn't have worked out. I've always seen myself as an *e-brigader*, because my engagement to conservation and preservation of the natural heritage has been with me my whole life. In other words, being authentic is fundamental.

Creativity and boldness were two other crucial elements in my path. In other words, believing in your utopias and finding ways of making them happen without leaving out the context. It's worth taking risks and being a pioneer. It's what I did when I opened the first Osklen store in the resort of Búzios, which sold winter coats with a differentiated quality that was soon perceived by foreign tourists that visited that little coastal town.

Originality is very important to the entrepreneur. Therefore, it's imperative to keep the perception channels wide open to be able to foresee the phenomena that are not yet evident to all. That's what I did when, going against the tendency of Brazilians to disqualify the national element, I valued the 'Brazilian soul', asserting the 'cool and Brazilian'. It's about cultivating the well-liked 'anticipatory consciousness', which enables us to be at the forefront as much as possible.

Challenges exist to be tried and faced. To overcome them, it is important to count on a group of good professionals who can also be acknowledged as counsellors. Knowing how to choose and knowing how to listen are tools of the utmost importance.

And, connecting it all, there's consistency with the values that are dear to me. Ethics and respect for otherness are what make my ideas, hopefully, inspiring to the readers of this book.

Oskar Metsavaht
Founder and CEO of OSKLEN, Rio de Janeiro, Brazil
November 2013

Acknowledgements

We would like to thank all those who, in the development process of the Best Performance in Sustainable Luxury in Latin America Award—at present evolving towards the Award in Sustainable Premium and Luxury at a global level—have contributed in some special way:

To the entrepreneurs who have participated in the first three years of the award—both nominees and winners—because, as creators of the future, they do not wait for the decisions that others can take in their place. They make conscious choices every day in accordance with their values.

To Professor Jem Bendell, currently Director of the Institute for Leadership and Sustainability, University of Cumbria, UK, who encouraged us to dive deeper into sustainable luxury from an academic and business point of view.

To Dana Thomas, author of the best seller, *Deluxe: How Luxury Lost its Luster*, one of the icons that sparked the debate on sustainable development in the luxury industry. Her contributions—as a member of the jury—have been important for the consolidation of the award.

To Ana Laura Torres, Co-Director of the Sustainable Textile Center, for her dedication in coordinating actions with all members of the jury in the first three years of the award. To Susana Saulquin, a Latin American reference in the field of sociology of fashion, who has been able to appraise this initiative and, with great effort, has participated as a member of the jury.

To Eduardo Escobedo, Director of the Responsible Ecosystems Sourcing Platform, a Collaborating Project of the Centre on Sustainable Consumption and Production, based in Geneva, whose contributions on the conservation and development of biodiversity have, undoubtedly, enriched this initiative.

We would like to thank, too, the following individuals who, with their work in the jury, have contributed to its consolidation: Christina Dean (Founder and CEO of Redress); Renata Mutis Black (Founder of Seven Bar Foundation); Summer Rayne Oakes (model-activist, author of bestselling style guide, *Style, Naturally*, and CEO/Co-founder of Source4Style) and Ian Doyle (co-author of *Uplifting the Earth: The Ethical Performance of Luxury Jewellery Brands Report*).

We also want to thank the sponsors who made possible the pleasant, emotive and inspirational award ceremonies and all the media that have spread this initiative over time.

M.A. Gardetti and M.E. Girón

María Eugenia Girón deserves a very special mention since, undoubtedly, she is the person who most supported and promoted this initiative with total and constant commitment. Her deep knowledge and experience in the luxury industry enabled her to make strategic contributions without which the award would not be what it is. Her business vision contrasts with my academic perspective, constantly challenging me, helping me to achieve deeper levels of thinking. She sees what I cannot see. A transparent, honest and integral person in the broadest dimension of these terms. Thanks, María Eugenia!

To José Testa for teaching me permanently through his gestures and actions.

Finally, my thanks go to my wife, Gloria, and my daughters, Macarena and Guadalupe, without whom I would not be who I am. Thanks to the three of them for their constant support and encouragement.

M.A. Gardetti

I am very grateful to Miguel Angel Gardetti, who involved me in the initiative of the Best Performance in Sustainable Luxury, when it was only an idea. Thanks for encouraging me always to challenge and contribute in a meaningful way. Working together is a learning experience and a joy.

Thanks to Oceana, the organization that protects the oceans worldwide. Being part of its board has made me more aware of the problems that affect out planet and of our responsibility to act. This book aims to be a step in this direction.

All this work could not be a reality without the energy and drive that I get from my family. They encourage me and support me to move further. They feel proud when I do.

M.E. Girón

Sustainable luxury:
Stories from the pioneers

María Eugenia Girón

> When Hellen Keller was asked whether it was worse not
> to see, to hear or to speak, she replied that the only thing
> worse than having no sight is not having a vision.

Sustainability is an opportunity for entrepreneurship

When Miguel Angel Gardetti got in touch with me over four years
ago to tell me about the sustainable luxury award, I was thrilled that
someone so far away was on the same wavelength as me. I was excited
that a textile engineer known for his studies on traceability and the
bottom of the pyramid had arrived at the conclusion that the premium and luxury industry could and should be a driving force behind
the necessary change. By this I mean the change in the way we consume. Because, as citizens first and foremost rather than consumers,

we are all concerned and anxious about the fate of our planet (Confino 2013).

I had reached the same conclusion as Miguel Angel almost simultaneously. After over 15 years professionally devoted to the luxury industry, I joined the international board of trustees of Oceana (www.oceana.org) in 2007. This decision opened up a new way of thinking for me, and represented the beginning of a discovery. Oceana is an environmental organisation that was created in 2000 with the purpose of protecting the oceans. Working towards clear, precise and measurable objectives, it has a first-class management team. Thanks to Oceana and the top scientists with which it collaborates, I was given the opportunity to reflect on and gain a better understanding of the problems and solutions that affect the environment. Listening to the team that leads Oceana's campaigns enabled me to understand the challenges we face as a society in bringing about this change. I became aware of the damage being done to our planet, and not only to the seas and oceans. I learned that a combination of rigorous, independently led science, legislative change, and support and impetus from civil society are the foundations we can build on in order to transform reality. And much more importantly, I learned that trends need not become our destiny and that it is up to us to change them. Our generation will be responsible. Our children and grandchildren will look us in the eye and say to us: You were there. What did you do to change it?

With Oceana I met many executives from the luxury industry. Like me, they had all come to the same conclusion. The most scarce and desirable commodity today is a healthy planet, one that brims with a diversity of life forms, clean air to breathe and clear water to enjoy. Essentially a planet just as we have known it or better, for our children and grandchildren and our grandchildren's grandchildren.

The most powerful brands in the luxury industry had already begun to take initiatives to protect this scarce commodity. Most of them were discreet about their programmes for promoting sustainability and social development. The greenwashing accusations the fashion industry and consumer products had suffered made them adopt a cautious approach. In some cases, certain brands had already jumped on board the 'green bandwagon', more as a PR tactic than out of a genuine interest for the cause. There was an immediate consumer backlash. Nobody was going to fool them about such serious and important issues! Thereafter, any initiative by a commercial brand, and particularly a premium brand, would be subject to public suspicion. Companies chose discretion: doing rather than appearing to be doing.

The success story of family brands Loro Piana and Ermenegildo Zegna in the Peruvian Andes, working with the vicuña, became a model for inspiration. Their work was the first proof that a threefold benefit—for the planet, for society and for businesses—was possible. Both companies worked with the local Andean communities. These communities were not only given training in breeding and shearing vicuñas, but also provided with and guaranteed purchase agreements for the wool over the long term. One of the results was that vicuña numbers recovered after the species had previously been on the brink of extinction. It is estimated that, in the 16th century, the total population of vicuñas in Peru, Bolivia, Chile and Argentina amounted to several million. During the period of European colonisation, however, the number of vicuñas started to go down. This became more marked during the 20th century. A census taken at the end of the 1960s showed that there were only between 5,000 and 10,000 vicuñas in Peru, and less than 2,000 in Bolivia, Chile and Argentina and, in 1970, the vicuña population had gone down to around 500 (Bonacic 2012). Yet, today, numbers have reached more than 350,000. This was the first example of active intervention by commercial brands allowing biodiversity to be recovered.

Another positive result of this programme was the economic development of the area. Many of the families who lived there previously had no alternative but to take the harsh decision to migrate to cities. In big cities such as Lima that were unprepared for the avalanche of people migrating from the countryside, they would become trapped in a circle of misery from which it was difficult to extract themselves. The chance of leading a decent life in their home town or village has allowed them to stay on there, work and even prosper.

The third advantage was for these brands, which were ensured the supply of a scarce and valuable raw material: vicuña wool. The vicuña, along with other South American camelids, comes from a family of animals that produces unusual fibres. Other examples are goats and rabbits which produce mohair, cashmere and angora. The extraordinary softness and lustre of this wool was what led it to be used in the textile industry over a century ago.

Italian family business Loro Piana, a brand that has been around for six generations, is the latest addition to the giant Louis Vuitton Moët Hennessy (LVMH). For €2 billion, LVMH acquired an 80% stake in the company in July 2013. For LVMH, an industry leader, the fundamental purpose of this strategic acquisition was to be able to control a century-old, prestigious brand dedicated to textiles and men's fashion. It has not been lost on anyone that this acquisition represents a clever move by LVMH in the chess game playing out in the luxury sector for control over raw materials. The acquisition of Loro Piana means controlling vicuña wool, a valuable and scarce resource. In the 1990s, the owning family could probably not have anticipated that the vicuña recovery programme initiated in the Andes would be a key instrument in creating strategic value for their brand.

Another example that demonstrates the luxury industry's involvement in the quest for sustainability can be seen with Tiffany jewellers. The American brand that has become entrenched in our collective imagination thanks to the legendary film, *Breakfast at Tiffany's*, starring the unforgettable Audrey Hepburn, has turned coral conservation into its own particular crusade. The production of jewellery is, among all the categories of luxury, the one that can be considered as most harmful to the environment. We only need remember that in order to extract the gold needed to produce a simple ring, nearly three tonnes of earth must be dug up and thousands of litres of water used.

Tiffany's campaigns alert us to the fact that the coral reefs, which generate a great deal of marine life, where fish spawn and young fish find protection, are threatened by destructive fishing techniques, particularly trawling. The iconic Fifth Avenue jeweller has not stopped at removing its range of coral jewellery. It has gone further, devoting shop window space to informing us, warning us and proposing solutions to this problem. Tiffany & Co. was created on Broadway in 1837, originally mainly producing desk accessories and gifts. Its international expansion would not begin until a century later. Today, first and foremost a jeweller, it has over 228 stores worldwide. Despite the size of Tiffany & Co., its decision not to use coral has a quite insignificant and marginal impact on the process of destruction of the coral reefs. However, the visibility it has given to this environmental problem is key: this aspirational brand, cooperating with organisations such as Oceana, has prompted people to seek a change in legislation in order to restrict the practice of trawling.

Why do well-established luxury brands, with thriving businesses and growing sales figures, take these initiatives in the name of sustainability? Why do brands that want to make us dream remind us of serious issues in the world? Why are we able to find more and more examples of similar projects? Is this a fad in the industry and all about keeping up? Is it because of the personal interests of their management staff? (Michael J. Kowalski, CEO of Tiffany for the last 12 years, is also a great fan of diving.) Is it because the DNA of a luxury brand contains the ability to anticipate dreams? Is it because brand managers are convinced that the new meaning of luxury is linked to sustainability?

I think the answer is good management. These steps are essential to ensure the survival and prosperity of a brand. Today no business project in the premium and luxury sector is able to thrive without incorporating sustainability as one of its values. Perhaps in some cases, a few years ago, greenwashing was the initial motivation. Fortunately, astute and committed citizens exposed the liars. They would not stand for brands using our problems as a weapon launched in the guise of a sustainable product. Those who manage the legendary brands we aspire to own know they must be aware of the aspirations of their customers at all times. They must discover them almost before the customers themselves, and must have a ready response, as did many of the luxury pioneers of the past who originated what then became legendary brands.

When Christian Dior presented his collection at his Avenue Montaigne salon in Paris in February 1947, he anticipated the dreams of many women. The new silhouette with wasp waist and wide skirts that used metres of fabric, reached straight out to many European women who wanted to leave behind the hardships of war and the frugal style they had to adopt during those years. They dreamed of a new future that Dior was able to crystallise in the silhouette that enthralled Editor-in-Chief of *Harper's Bazaar*, Carmel Snow: 'It's quite a revolution, dear Christian. Your dresses have such a new look' (the 'new look' as it came to be known; see Voguepedia website). *Vogue* magazine said the presentation was a 'direct, unblushing plan to make women extravagantly, romantically, eyelash-battingly female'. Christian Dior had a ready response to the aspirations and dreams of his customers. 'Women, with their sure instincts, realised that my intention was to make them not just more beautiful but also happier', he later reflected (see Voguepedia website). Luxury brands, creators and the pioneers of premium who solve the equation of traceability and sustainability are carrying out a similar exercise of anticipating our dreams today. Because for a luxury brand one of the keys to success is knowing how to anticipate our dreams.

When Miguel Angel Gardetti told me about the award in the autumn of 2009, he explained that the purpose was to give visibility to entrepreneurs who were starting out on this path. After experiencing the first ripples of enjoyment, excitement and enthusiasm, I faced the anxiety of the unknown. Would there be enough business initiatives for prizes to be awarded in several categories, and enough candidates?

Would there be sufficient critical mass and entrepreneurship? Would we find many examples of entrepreneurial projects that took this route and achieved success? Would we be anticipating a trend?

The good news is that we discovered there were enough projects and entrepreneurs. We discovered much to our delight that anywhere from Los Angeles to London, Madrid, Monaco, Sao Paulo or Buenos Aires, premium and luxury companies are redefining the meaning of luxury. They devote all their effort, enthusiasm and vision to updating the meaning of luxury so that it is aligned with the new values of sustainability sought and almost demanded by customers and citizens. We found that all the entrepreneurship occurring in this sector incorporates both the digital world and technology in general, in an attempt to revise and update values.

During the three years that the awards have taken place we have analysed more than 50 projects. All of them are projects with international roots and an international perspective, led by entrepreneurs with vision. Aïny, Pachacuti, Positive Luxury, We are Knitters, the IOU Project, Big Blue Bike, Elvis & Kresse, Bottletop and Estancia Peuma Hue are among the pioneers. We have chosen them to appear in this book because together they represent the diversity of the countries from which they originate, the product categories, experiences and different profiles. All are pioneers, not only because they have taken the plunge and have set off on a journey through uncharted territory, but because they are actually establishing themselves in this new territory. They all represent thriving, growing businesses that have already got through the first moments of uncertainty, proving their viability. They will now live through their first winters and have to fend off their enemies. Their vision remains unquestioned. They have shown that what they offer is part of our dreams and aspirations.

Traceability: the starting point

Many of the pioneering projects described in this book originated from the aim of ensuring that the development, manufacturing and sale of the products or services they offered had a positive impact on the planet and on people. They start out from the assumption that if they give visibility to the supply chain of their products, they thereby reveal their strongest values.

Where do things come from? What is the story behind the products we consume or the services we use? What footprints have these products left on the environment and on the people who create, manufacture, sell or consume them? The journey to the past to understand where a product comes from, its components, raw materials and their extraction, is what is known as traceability. It is a tortuous, difficult journey. The first step we take back is an immediate one: meeting our suppliers; the second one is already more complicated, because we have to investigate the suppliers of our suppliers; and the third is a cloud of confusion in which companies routinely lose the trail. On this journey to discover the footprint left in the world by the products we happily and unwittingly consume, we have come up against environmental implications and ethical issues on numerous occasions. We only need recall the recent fire and collapse of an apparel factory in Bangladesh that resulted in the death of over 800 workers. Our blindness is such that we convince ourselves that cotton shirts can be sold at €3 without any social or environmental cost.

Our first priority as consumers has been to find out where the food we eat comes from, as this has a direct impact on our health. We are concerned about our own health and well-being, as well as that of others, more than the planet. This is why the first mention of the issue of traceability focused on the food industry. Recent developments and scientific reports have stimulated this concern and interest in the traceability of what we put in our mouths. Inexplicable scandals have occurred: in the UK, there was an epidemic of **BSE** or **mad cow disease** in 1986, when scientists determined that the disease was brought about by the supplementary feeding of cattle with sheep and goat offal; or Oceana's recent report on the fish fraud in the US, which shows that about one-third of fish samples analysed nationwide were mislabelled according to US Food and Drug Administration (FDA) guidelines (www. oceana.org); or medical reports on the increased likelihood of developing tumours due to some of the fertilisers and substances used in intensive farming.

International movements such as 'slow food', an interest in local farming and the rise of organic farming have arisen from this drive for health. In short, we have a new category of healthy, organic products and a new luxury segment in the food industry. This segment is one of the fastest growing in the luxury food category, according to the latest report by the reputable Altagamma foundation.

If our primary concern is food, it is closely followed by cosmetics. Its external use has health implications for us. The next issue would be fabrics as they also come into contact with our skin. The most recent report by the aforementioned Altagamma shows that sales figures for 'eco-luxury' goods account for 3% of the total sales volume of personal luxury items, quantified at €212 billion (Fondazione Altagamma 2012).

Traceability has become the most accurate approach to sustainability. The concept of sustainability is not easy to understand. What does sustainability mean? It is about using resources in a responsible way. It is about giving back to society or the planet what we take from it. How can this be measured in terms of the things we buy? During a conference where I was presenting my book, *Inside Luxury*, and was trying to explain this concept, someone asked me what a sustainable watch was. I referred to the notion of traceability. This is much clearer and easier to understand.

For our pioneers, sustainable premium and luxury also mean clear traceability. For We are Knitters, Pachacuti or Big Blue Bike, their vision is based on the responsible use of raw materials. This is, respectively, wool, Panama straw or alpaca fibres, produced or grown in a sustainable manner that involves the local communities in the creation of the wealth generated. For Elvis & Kresse and Bottletop, their response to traceability is to use waste material. Bags and accessories made with material from fire hoses or ring pulls from drink cans are the weapons of our pioneers in waging our war against rubbish. Aïny comes at it from a different angle and suggests that biodiversity be maintained out of necessity, offering us cosmetics based on the endangered Amazon biodiversity precisely in order to protect this biodiversity. Aïny's hypothesis is that if we look for commercial uses in botanical species, they will not disappear because we will rely on them as a source of wealth.

Doing well by doing good: is it realistic or wishful thinking?

All the pioneers featured in this book manage businesses that are sustainable in every sense of the word. They are companies that can sustain themselves by generating sales and cash.

There was a time when unrealistic eco-fanatics believed that proposing a more sustainable product would be reason enough to drive sales. They forgot that customers will not give up quality, style or fashion appeal or a competitive price for a sustainable product.

This was confirmed in the early results of some sustainable consumption research conducted by Havas Media on this subject in 2010. The findings showed that 48% of consumers were willing to pay more for products produced in an environmentally and socially responsible way, but 64% viewed companies' communications about sustainability as 'marketing tools' (Populus Research/Strategy 2009). The Havas Media research also revealed that 86% of people considered sustainability issues when deciding what to buy and that with the same conditions of price and quality, 80% of people under the age of 35 would choose the sustainable option. To come up with the findings, the firm surveyed around 20,000 consumers in ten markets, covering more than 50 brands across eight different sectors.

In this regard, Amy du Pon, Head of Strategic Planning at Havas, told the Sustainable Brands '13 Conference in San Diego: 'In an age of transparency and empowerment, brands are not meeting people's requirements. People expect large companies to be involved in social problems and their quality of life'.[1]

Additional research on company performance, such as the *2013 Small Business Sustainability Report: The Big Green Opportunity for Small Business in the US* (Green America, the Association for Enterprise Opportunity and EcoVentures International 2013), reported that for small businesses defined as having five or fewer work associates (representing 88% of all businesses in the US) the sale of green products outpaced the sale of their conventional products.

The relationship between the consumer, brands and society has changed forever. In the context of a planet that will have 9 billion people by 2050, we need to solve the sustainability equation. Resources matter! Up to now the sustainable products economy has been pigeon-holed, marginal and very limited. I am convinced that it will reposition itself faster now, moving to the forefront as consumers start to care more and more. All these signs confirm that we are moving away from the traditional model of mass consumption as we have known it in past decades. This model has reached its limits. There is no way back.

However, what we see today is still a gap between the attitude to consumer choices and actual behaviour when making these choices. The gap will close as the supply side gets better, and this is improving rapidly. The pioneers included in this book are some of the best examples of how companies are working hard and managing to close this gap.

The products offered by the brands included here cover a wide price range, from €19 to €1,300. They all compete in their categories

---

1 www.sustainablebrands.com/events/sb13

with top companies and brands. They know that their products must at least match the quality and design of the alternatives and provide the additional value of sustainability. Their products are, at least, as competitive as the best. When customers choose them over alternatives it is because they provide the additional value of environmental and social responsibility, which makes them superior.

All the companies that are included are growing and expect to continue to do so. They started with resources of their own and from their closest circles. Some of them have already attracted capital from professional investors and expect to initiate new rounds of funding. Others I know of have not gone down this route because they want to strengthen the concept before getting new partners on board.

All of them started out as end-consumer-oriented businesses (B2C). In other words, their vision was to deliver better products and services to customers around the world. They relied on the Internet to get their products to wherever their customers were. The IOU Project, Elvis & Kresse or Pachacuti, projects focused on very different categories (fashion, bags and hats, respectively), went into the business with the world in mind. And they succeeded. Later on, they discovered that it was not only consumers who were interested in the sustainable products they offered, but there were also other brands that wanted to follow the sustainability path and did not know how to go about it. They asked them for help. In almost all cases our pioneers are now selling their technology and their know-how to other brands that also want to incorporate the value of sustainability.

So, entrepreneurs in the world of responsible luxury and premium have operated in two different ways:

- During the first stage they created products that anticipated the dreams (and the needs) of their customers, in which traceability was an additional value. They developed companies based on business models that work, in addition to being committed to the social and environmental impact.

- In the second stage of development, they are offering and selling their methodology to other companies. In other words, they have developed a line of business geared towards other businesses (B2B), which they did not anticipate at the beginning. The IOU Project does this by licensing its technology as a software company. Pachacuti is developing a house brand for other players in the men's fashion world. Elvis & Kresse is looking for franchisees around the world to implement the methodology they have successfully developed in the UK.

Let us not lose sight of the fact that the goal of these entrepreneurs is to better the world through economically viable projects, the former being a key element. This is why they do not hesitate to share their knowledge and experience with those who may contribute to their dream with speed and success.

For Kresse Wesling, Elvis & Kresse's aim is to rid the world of waste. They began with used fire hoses that would otherwise have been consigned to the scrapheap. They transformed them into bags, accessories and belts which they sold online or at top sales outlets such as Harrods in London. They built an aspirational brand that was then splashed all over the fashion editorials. The company that started with Elvis, and that they called Elvis & Kresse, now manages to recycle all the fire hoses in the UK otherwise destined to be thrown in landfills each year. This was their first step to success. But as the problem still exists, they have already started other lines of business using other materials. Their latest obsession is with the metallic meshes used in the microphones of mobile phones. They are keen to pass on their hose recycling idea to other countries around the world, to other entrepreneurs with the knowledge and local connections that are likely to be more effective there. They will provide all the technology and will share their experiences. Anything that can help them in the battle to rid the world of rubbish is highly welcomed.

For Kavita Parmar, co-founder of the IOU Project, together with her husband Iñigo, the goal is for the artisans of the world to regain their dignity. They started with the Madras weavers in India. She says:

> They told us their stories, took us to their homes and introduced us to their families. They put us in touch with the artisans whose products we wanted, making this relationship transparent. And the feeling was that the artisan who is normally so far removed from us was making a product just for me, one that was unique, different from the rest and that I would be able to personally enjoy (personal conversation).

The weavers or artisans felt that their work was appreciated and enjoyed. They also share, in a fair and balanced way, the price the customer has paid. They have used all the technology at their disposal for this purpose: video, QR codes, pictures and so on, and have developed their own technology to make this possible. They are now sharing this know-how with extremely well-known brands to help promote the development of responsible products. This brings them closer to their goal of restoring dignity to the craftsmen of the world.

For Daniel Joutard, founder and director of Aïny, Savoirs des Peuples, the goal is to protect plant biodiversity and the respect for traditional knowledge. To this end he has developed a methodology for well-being and a line of cosmetics. The products are based on a combination of Western science and traditional wisdom on the many species of plants that can be used for healing. Creating a new brand of cosmetics in France, the most competitive market in the world, requires conviction and courage. Hence, Aïny has not hesitated to use its technology and its Parisian laboratory to develop formulas for other companies, even if this was something that they did not envisage to begin with.

For Carry Somers, founder and director of Pachacuti, the purpose is to lead the way and set an example of how to integrate sustainability into the fashion supply chain. Her message is clear: genuine luxury needs to incorporate social and environmental responsibility without compromising on design and quality. She began her journey as a pioneer in what is known as ethical fashion in 1992. She calls her project Pachacuti, which means upside-down world in the Quechua language. Her weapon is the Panama hat, an object and symbol of outright exploitation in the past. The advantage of the fibre used is that it can be harvested every 30 days for 100 years from the same plant. Nothing is thrown away because what is not used for weaving the hats is used to make roofs.

Pachacuti gives its weavers long-term contracts and fair wages for their work, bringing back dignity to the trade. Following the economic development it ignited, it launched social development, health and education programmes. Pachacuti today makes collections for other brands. These commercial partners give impetus to the work initiated and bring Carry nearer to her primary goal.

For Pepita and Alberto of 'We are Knitters', inspiration came from the work of Loro Piana in the Andes. Their aim is to recover the highest quality Peruvian wool. When they started, they were witnessing a trend that was spreading around the world and encouraging young people to return to the idea of 'do it yourself'. Even knitting, which my generation associated with idle grannies, had turned into an aspirational activity for young urbanites. Their company was created from this premise. First they began by building a community of fans that united this passion. Then they offered them a set of needles, wools and patterns. And above all they handed them the dream of looking like the 'cool' tribe who wore big jumpers, hats and scarves. As they went along, the wool led them on to cotton and Spain became a springboard for moving to other countries. What stayed with them was the close working relationship with the communities of Peruvian shepherds and weavers, something which continues to bring an identity, value and a meaning to their project.

For Diana Verde Nieto, founder and director of Positive Luxury, the purpose of her business is to give visibility to those working towards sustainability and to provide guidance to those who want to act responsibly. This led her to the conclusion that removing the word sustainability from ostracism and rejection would be a way of making it attractive and aspirational. She therefore chose the field of premium products and included the term 'positive' in the name of her project. She was persuaded that she had to bestow this term with a sense of positivity, transparency and style . . . And she did. Today, the Positive Luxury website features more than 400 premium brands and has 120,000 users. In the beginning they received support from some of the pioneers in this book. Today Diana takes this matter to international forums such as the World Economic Forum, where she leads debates on growth, innovation and entrepreneurship.

For Cameron and Oliver, the founders of Bottletop, the goal is to recycle all the soft drink can ring pulls on the planet, a quest that brought them into contact with artisans, with proud hands skilled at making beautiful products. Their mission expanded to include the women who made up their artisan network base, providing them with an education, training and a new way of life. Their social achievements are plain to see as they have created jobs in depressed areas, such as the 40 jobs in the poorest area of El Salvador. Their environmental achievements are even clearer; they have managed to save 10 million aluminium ring pulls from ending up in landfill sites.

For Shudhan Kohli, founder and director of Big Blue Bike (BBB), the goal is to change the world and to make an impact. The instrument for this is alpaca wool and fashion. During the early stages he tried to fit in with the standards of this industry: trade fairs, seasons, deadlines . . . But today his company is pivoting towards a business model directly aimed at the end consumer. The cogs in the unstoppable fashion machine have difficulties in incorporating innovative concepts such as BBB. Shudhan is not giving up and knows that he has started out on a long journey, just like his ancestors who travelled from India to East Africa. His grandfather developed companies in the food sector and the construction industry and he and his father were educated in the US. The enterprising and searching spirit in his family inspires and drives him. For those with a vision no road is too long and there are no boundaries.

Evelyn Hoter, founder and director of Estancia Peuma Hue, intended to live in one of the most beautiful places in the world, where she spent the happiest moments of her childhood: Bariloche, Argentina. But she did not want to live there in any old way. Her aim was to do so in complete harmony with the environment. The mission she set herself was for future generations to be able to enjoy it as she had been able to. This is how her company, a hotel, came about. It offers guests the chance to enjoy their stay there while protecting the natural environment around it. Peuma Hue proffered a solution to the prevailing economic model, a model that today is causing the destruction and abuse of resources, something that is incompatible with a finite and limited planet. And what is more, it turned into a flourishing business. It now has a turnover of US$650,000 and is making a profit. The project has improved the quality of life of the people who live and work there, as well as protecting the clean air and clear water that it was at risk of losing.

For all our pioneers, the financial prosperity of their businesses is a means to achieving their ultimate goal more quickly. They are selfish in that they are generous with their secrets. It is a giving kind of selfishness. This message from Bobby Sager, an active philanthropist who has spent years promoting the shift, impressed me the first time I heard it at the YPO (Young Presidents' Organization) Global Leadership Conference 2013: 'Be selfish, go help someone'.

Financial summary

The financial figures of our pioneers are summarised in Table 1. We do not just look at commonly measured data such as sales figures and margins. We also include in Table 1 the social and/or environmental benefits that have been achieved. They know, as we do, that what is not measured is not managed.

Table 1 **Financial figures for the Sustainable Luxury Pioneers**

	Ainy	Pachacuti	Positive Luxury	We Are Knitters	The IOU Project	BBB	Elvis&Kresse	Bottletop	Peuma Hue
Size (sales)	€500,000.00	£450,000 (2012)	400 brands, 120,000 users, K score 67%	€350,000.00	$1,500,000.00	$15,000.00	£350,000.00	4 employees in UK, 20 in Brazil and 20 part-time	$636,000.00
Profit	yes	yes, break even at £300,000	Break even expected year 2015	Break even 2014	Break even 2013	Break even at $20,000	profitable from year one 2008	Break even expected in three years	Break even at 30% occupancy: Currently 35%
Expected growth based on previous years	10%	15%	100%	40%	100%		20%	NA	25%
Average price	€19-62	£55-450	NA	€40	$38-170	$235.00	£18-300	£200-1000	$245.00
Distribution	B2B	B2C, B2B; private label	NA	B2C	B2C	B2B/B2C	B2C/B2B	B2B, dep stores	NA
Investment	€300,000.00	NA	NA	€170,000	$2,500,000.00	$10,000.00	£40000	NA	$500,000.00
Investors	founder+FF	founder	founder +FF	founder+BA	founder+FF	founder	founder	founders +others	founders +FF

	Aïny	Pachacuti	Positive Luxury	We Are Knitters	The IOU Project	BBB	Elvis&Kresse	Bottletop	Peuma Hue
Social impact	50 families + indirect	Prices paid to producers increased by average 21% well above cost of living. Other social investments amount to more than £2300 in 2010	As we help people make better choices, they exercise their consumer power to buy brands that are investing in a better world	Development of local communities in Peru	Building prosperity chains, where products are embedded with full traceability from artisan to consumer. Pride and higher prices for craftspeople	Provided employment for 30 women over a cycle of 3 months each year	50% of profits are donated to charities relevant to the waste used	Employment for over 40 people in one of the poorest neighborhoods in El Salvador	Enhances quality of life
	Biodiversity, 70% reduction of CO2 emissions from cold process	45% reduction of CO2 consumption over 5 years. Switched to 100% renewable energy	As we help people make better choices, people exercise their consumer power to buy brands that are investing in a better world	Locally produced wool	Locally grown cotton	No chemical waste, reduced water consumption. Delivering a product free from environmental costs	Reclaimed 250 tonnes of waste	Saved 10 million ring pulls	Environmental preservation

Making sustainability aspirational: back to the true meaning of luxury

> People often ask me how they can eat fish in a sustainable way. Sardines are a good answer. There has been no better inspiration to eat sardines than recipes from Michelin-starred chefs, which have made them aspirational. That is the power of luxury (Dr Daniel Pauly, University of British Columbia, board member of Oceana).

The luxury industry is based on innovation, creativity and excellence. Its aim is to provide the best products and experiences for well-informed, educated, sophisticated, demanding and discerning clients. However, the term 'best' has a different meaning for all of us, and this meaning changes and evolves with time. A century ago, the best kind of luggage was a trunk with a flat lid, covered with waterproof material. It was developed by Louis Vuitton, and was suitable for transatlantic voyages. This is a product that is not relevant for the needs of people today.

We live in a world where resources are scarce, the planet is deteriorating and poverty is increasing. The best products today are those that not only are beautifully designed and well made, but are produced from the finest materials. The meaning of 'best product' has changed forever.

In 2013, the best products are those that can claim a history of clean traceability, reaching beyond their tangible beauty. To represent true contemporary luxury, the best products need to be socially and environmentally responsible. It is impossible to speak today of luxury without integrating the notion of sustainability into the equation. The luxury domain can only be claimed nowadays by companies and brands that act responsibly towards the environment and towards people.

The premium and luxury industry benefits from discerning customers, good margins and international visibility, all of which make sustainability aspirational. Entrepreneurs understand this opportunity.

Aspirational sustainability is a realistic way of taking the lead and initiating the necessary transformation of consumer patterns, of which our planet is in dire need. Luxury is regaining its true meaning of products made to last for ever by people who enjoyed making them.

Bibliography

Bonacic, C. (2012) 'Vicuña Ecology and Management', Ecology.Info, www.ecología.info/vicugna-2.htm, accessed 9 December 2013.

Confino, J. (2013) 'Consumers believe brands can have positive impact but are failing to do so', Guardian Sustainable Business, www.theguardian.com/sustainable-business/consumers-brands-positive-impact-failing, accessed 9 December 2013.

Fondazione Altagamma (2012) *Worldwide Markets Monitor* (Milan: Fondazione Altagamma).

Green America, the Association for Enterprise Opportunity and EcoVentures International (2013) *2013 Small Business Sustainability Report: The Big Green Opportunity for Small Business in the US (Washington, DC: Green America, the Association for Enterprise Opportunity and EcoVentures International)*.

'New Look', Voguepedia, www.vogue.com/voguepedia/New_Look, accessed 9 December 2013.

Populus Research/Strategy (2009) 'Havas rates companies' sustainability credentials', www.research-live.com/news/havas-rates-companies-sustainability-credentials/3006252.article, accessed 9 December 2013.

Wikipedia 'Encefalopatía espongiforme bovina', http://es.wikipedia.org/wiki/Encefalopat%C3%ADa_espongiforme_bovina, accessed 9 December 2013.

Stories from the social pioneers in the sustainable luxury sector:

A conceptual vision

Miguel Angel Gardetti

Luxury and sustainable development

Klaus Heine (2011) defines luxury as something desirable and more than a necessity. This definition, though relative depending on the cultural, economic or regional contexts which transform luxury into an ambiguous concept, shows—for some researchers such as Saskia Scheibel (no date)—the absurd aspect of this industry. However luxury has been a sign of prosperity, power and social status since ancient times (Kapferer and Basten 2010). Thus, luxury is a matter of seeing and being seen. 'Seeing' as a search of the last distinctive signifiers that can be used to 'be seen' in different distinctive group processes (Mortelmans 2005). Christopher L. Berry in his work, *The Idea of Luxury*, from 1994—one of the most interesting and comprehensive pieces on the concept of luxury particularly its intellectual history—establishes that luxury has changed throughout time and that it reflects social norms and aspirations.

True elements of (authentic) luxury rely on the search for beauty, refinement, innovation, purity, the well-made, what remains, the essence of things, the ultimate best (Girón 2012).

However this luxury has given way to the *new luxury* through its democratisation (massification?) that occurred when family and artisanal luxury companies sagged against the large conglomerates which had a strong focus on economic aspects. Dana Thomas, in her work, *Deluxe: How Luxury Lost its Luster* (2007), was very clear about the consequences of this process: 'the luxury industry ... has sacrificed its integrity, undermined its products, stained its history and deceived its customers'. It is that the image—neither the reputation nor the legitimacy—was the way, and the marketing the function. As early as 1999 Robert H. Frank stated in his book, *Luxury Fever: Weighing the Cost of Excess*, the need to minimise the culture of 'excess' to restore the true values of life. And this is in line with the World Commission on Environment and Development (WCED 1987) report, *Our Common Future*, also known as the Brundtland Report, which defines sustainable development as the development model that allows us to meet present needs, without compromising the ability of future generations to meet their own needs. According to this report the three pillars of sustainability would be 'people, profit and planet'. The main objective of this development model is to raise the quality of life by maximising the productive potential of the ecosystem in the long term, through technologies appropriate for these purposes. The Brundtland Report can be considered as the starting point of discussions on sustainable development, thus constituting an important political change (Mebratu 1998). Yet at the World Summit on Sustainable Development in Johannesburg in 2002, this evolved into 'people, planet and prosperity' where the term prosperity is broader than profit. It is a notion of the world deeply different from the one that dominates our current thinking and includes satisfying basic human needs such as justice, freedom and dignity (Ehrenfeld 1999).

Some concerns in 2007 . . . The beginning of sustainable luxury?

In addition to Dana Thomas's book, Caroline Weber from the *New York Times* states in her article 'The Devil Sells Prada', published on 26 August 2007: 'luxury brands were guarantors of value and integrity, they are now markers that point toward nothing, guiding the consumer on a road to nowhere'. Towards the end of 2007 a documentary by RAI 3 entitled 'Slaves of Luxury' showed in depth the supply chain of Italian luxury fashion brands. The documentary showed cases of Chinese illegal immigrants in Italy making accessories for Dolce & Gabbana and Prada. The audience was estimated at 4 million people and the RAI's internet forums collapsed (Ilari and Zargani 2007). In 2007 Roberto Saviano published *Gomorrah* which reports that a white suit worn by one of the world's most famous women, Angelina Jolie, on the red carpet at the Oscars, was made by someone employed by organised criminals accused of multiple murders.

The report *Deeper Luxury*—published in November 2007 by WWF and written by Jem Bendell and Anthony Kleanthous—points out that the consumers of luxury products and services are motivated by aspirations and these encompass deep values including environmental and social issues. Luxury, according to Kleanthous (2011), is becoming less exclusive and less wasteful and more about helping people to express their deepest values. So, sustainable luxury is a return to the essence of luxury with its ancestral meaning, to the thoughtful purchase, to the artisan manufacturing, to the beauty of materials in its broadest sense and to the respect for social and environmental issues. Sustainable luxury would not only be the vehicle for more respect for the environment and social development, but it will also be synonymous to culture, art and innovation of different nationalities, maintaining the legacy of local craftsmanship (Gardetti 2011). This deeper approach requires and will require a relentless search for knowledge and discovery and mainly for understanding. Thus, the luxury consumer will be identified as one who has both the means and the motivation to ensure care for the environment and for other people to improve their quality of life (Bendell and Kleanthous 2007).

Sustainable luxury and entrepreneurship

There are people with a profound connection with environmental and social issues and who are well motivated to 'break' the rules and promote disruptive solutions to these issues; most of them are entrepreneurs. These individuals have a number of different roles to play in entrepreneurship and innovation, from the imaginative act of setting up a new venture. This involves cognitive and motivational characteristics. We are also talking about the radical aspect and, in the context of this volume, many sustainability-improving innovations which tend to require some level of technological radicalness are carried out by smaller firms, reflecting the theoretically and empirically well-established negative association between firm size and the level of technological radicalness of an innovation (Schumpeter 1934; Markides and Geroski 2005; Schaltegger and Wagner 2011). They are less constrained by existing realities than larger organisations, have less vested interest in the status quo and have less to lose and more to gain from innovation (O'Malley 2011).

But, in addition, to achieve a profound social change, the role of personal values is very important: idealistic values regarding environmental and social goals can be translated into value economic assets (Dixon and Clifford 2007). Entrepreneurs have a transformational leadership behaviour, inspiring and guiding the fundamental transformation that sustainability requires (Egri and Herman 2000).

And, in practice, this was the perception throughout the first three editions of the **Best Performance in Sustainable Luxury in Latin America Award**[2] organised by the **Center for Studies on Sustainable Luxury since 2011,**[3] which enabled organisers to build sound relationships with entrepreneurs from the luxury sector, such as, Diana Verde Nieto (Positive Luxury, UK), Oliver Wayman and Cameron Saul (Bottletop, UK), Kavita Parmar (The IOU Project, Spain), Carry Somers (Pachacuti, UK) and Daniel Joutard (Aïny, France), among others. Most of these projects have developed an inclusive supply chain with poor and vulnerable Latin American communities and show respect for their local culture and, in turn, develop environmentally sustainable products.

Transformational leaders

The examples contained in this book have been created and developed by transformational leaders that inspire, provide intellectual stimulus and care deeply about people and the environment. And leadership and inspiration are crucial in the move towards sustainability in the

2 The main purpose of the award is to acknowledge the culture and practice of sustainability in the luxury sector (in Latin America), and hence of their communication, in order to encourage a 'more sustainable' and therefore 'more authentic' luxury. This award can be granted to companies and entrepreneurs whose origin might not be Latin American but the impact of their actions is generated in this region.

3 The mission of the Center for Studies on Sustainable Luxury is to assist luxury companies in their transition to sustainability, thus encouraging sustainable business practices across all areas of the organisation and its supply chain. To this end, academic learning and research will become vital for future 'sustainable' leaders. This means taking a broader view to ensure that social and environmental issues are completely integrated into the decision-making process.

luxury sector. Clearly this relates to the concept of 'tempered radicals' developed by Meyerson and Scully (1995). The authors define it as,

> individuals who identify with and are committed to their organizations, and are committed to a cause, community, or ideology that is fundamentally different from, and possibly at odds with the dominant culture ... The ambivalent stance of these individuals creates a number of special challenges and opportunities.

If the goal is to achieve a smooth transition to a healthier economy and society, we must move quickly to establish the credibility of alternative ways of doing business and challenge the legitimacy of the status quo (O'Malley 2011).

Emerging Davids versus Established Goliaths: a conceptual vision from the Best Performance in Sustainable Luxury in Latin America Award[4]

Within the luxury industry, it can be observed that new companies— Emerging Davids—are based on values (Bendell 2012) and this is attractive for a select number of consumers since this kind of company can generate a big impact through its potential for reaching a larger market (Villiger *et al.* 2000). These Davids have an active attitude based on a very pronounced values approach with the intention to generate social and environmental changes (Hockerts and Wüstenhagen 2009; see Figure 1). For that reason they revalue the local culture and respect native peoples. They are the Davids in search of the Goliaths, a situation that is occurring particularly in Latin America.

---

4 The expression 'Emerging Davids versus Established Goliaths' was adapted from the *Emerging Davids versus Greening Goliaths* work developed by Kai Hockerts and Rolf Wüstenhagen in 2009.

The established international brands rarely go beyond incremental innovation since they are anchored to the usual thinking structure.

How do the established brands respond to this situation? A number of recent reports indicate that the established brands' progress towards sustainability is slow: for example *Deeper Luxury* (Bendell and Kleanthous 2007), *Uplifting the Earth: The Ethical Performance of Luxury Jewellery Brands* (Doyle and Bendell 2011) and 'Style Over Substance: Why Ethics Are Not in Fashion for Designer Labels' (Bryony Moore for the Ethical Consumer Research Association 2011) in which 20 luxury brands are assessed under a series of criteria such as environment, testing on animals, furs, gold and diamonds, rights of workers and activity in politics, among others. Even though some brands have a proactive attitude towards the challenge of sustainability, it is observed that, in general, the industry reacts to what the market and consumers are demanding (see Figure 1). In this sense, some initiatives have begun to appear. One example is that of Loro Piana, the highly regarded Italian company, which organised a consortium including Condortips, a textile producer from Arequipa (southern Peru), Lanerie Agnona SpA, an Italian knit fabric producer (at present owned by Ermenegildo Zegna), and the Government of Peru. In the agreement, the consortium also committed to fund an association of breeders with two goals in mind:

- **Improve production.** Breeders are usually from native aboriginal communities of the region who want to emigrate to the large urban centre of Lima (the capital city of Peru) and kill the animals to make quick profits.

- **Teach conservation techniques.** Vicuñas were declared an endangered species since in 1974 there were only 6,000 animals left.

As a result, the vicuña population has currently reached 180,000 animals and it may grow to 1 million over the next 10 years, depending on the fibre demand. There is a clear impact on local communities:

their daily income has increased four times against the level before the project, they stayed in the region, and they have developed new capabilities.

In turn and since 2009 Ermenegildo Zegna has been developing a similar project with 200 aboriginal families from the Picotani community. They have developed a channelling system to improve watering capacity in the fields where vicuñas live, and they have raised the level of a lagoon to enhance the water reservoir in the area. In addition, they are building an 11 km road for easier communication between breeders.

The documentary 'PPR Home' by the PPR Group, with a €10 million investment (Bendell 2012), promotes a new business paradigm based on creativity and innovation for the achievement of sustainability: 'PPR Home moves beyond the conventional CSR approach' (PPR HOME 2011). According to some authors, such as Jem Bendell (2012), the success that PPR can get from this documentary can be as important as the innovations of the Emerging Davids presented in this book. The essential question here is whether the disruptive innovation can be performed in a group of this size.

In the jewellery sector, Cartier works with the Italian gold mining company Goldlake operating in Honduras through its subsidiary Eurocantera, which combines zero waste from its mine and processing facilities, mitigation of impacts on ecosystems and natural habitats and the use of zero-pollution technologies. In order to implement these goals, Goldlake combines a modern alluvial gold mine (meaning the gold is found in water, close to the surface, requiring no blasting into rock) with small-scale miners who use traditional methods of panning gold (Bendell 2012).

Another interesting example is Hermès, which 'discovered' the value of craftsmanship and found new life for its products, disseminating the ancestral tenangos embroideries. For the researcher Carmen Lorenzo Monterrubio (2008) the tenangos are pieces of textile art that identify the Otomi region of Tenango de Doria, in Hidalgo (Mexico) and have become the codices of the present. In them, the community leaves the testimony of everyday life, in which their rites and ceremonies, the field, the games, the homes and the region, among other things, are reflected. This project was born around 2009 once the international firm became interested in working with the best craftsmen of Mexico.

Figure 1 **Emerging Davids and Established Goliaths depending on two variables**

Source: author

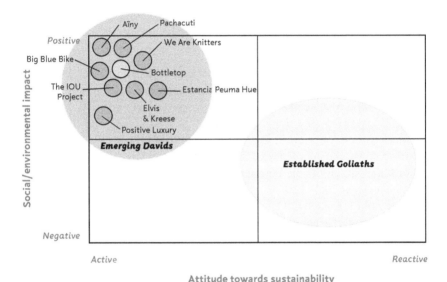

Conclusions

While, as we have seen, established brands—Goliaths—are slowly progressing, the cases presented in this book—the Emerging Davids—represent new business norms and the expectation that business should create and not destroy social and environmental value. It is this creative and disruptive type of change that will help us to move more quickly and effectively to transformational behaviour. Jen Morgan

(2011) expressed this: 'To leapfrog ahead, we need pioneering and brave people, communities and organizations who are willing and able to challenge that status quo and to experiment for change'. In this book you can read about people that, as creators of the future, do not wait for the decisions that others can take in their place. They start by making conscious choices every day in accordance with their values.

Bibliography

Bendell, J. (2012) *Elegant Disruption: How Luxury and Society Can Change Each-Other for Good* (Queensland: Griffith University).

Bendell, J., and A. Kleanthous (2007) *Deeper Luxury* (London: WWF).

Berry, C.J. (1994) *The Idea of Luxury: A Conceptual and Historical Investigation* (New York: Cambridge University Press).

Dixon, S.E.A., and A. Clifford (2007) 'Ecopreneurship: A New Approach to Managing the Triple Bottom Line', *Journal of Organizational Change Management* 20.3: 32645.

Doyle, I., and J. Bendell (2011) 'Uplifting the Earth: The Ethical Performance of Luxury Jewellery Brands', www.lifeworth.com/consult/2011/06/uplifting, accessed December 2012.

Egri, C.P., and S. Herman (2000) 'Leadership in North American Environmental Sector: Values, Leadership Styles and Contexts of Environmental Leaders and their Organizations', *Academy of Management Journal* 43.4: 523-53.

Ehrenfeld, J.R. (1999) 'Cultural Structure and the Challenge of Sustainability', in K. Sexton, A.A. Marcus, K.W. Easter and T.D. Burckhardt (eds.), *Better Environmental Decisions: Strategies for Governments, Businesses, and Communities* (Washington, DC: Island Press).

Frank, R.H. (1999) *Luxury Fever: Weighing the Cost of Excess* (Princeton, NJ: Princeton University Press).

Gardetti, M.A. (2011) Sustainable Luxury in Latin America, conference dictated at the Seminar Sustainable Luxury & Design, Instituto de Empresa (Business School), Madrid, Spain.

Girón, M.E. (2012) *Diccionario LID sobre Lujo y Responsabilidad (Madrid: Editorial LID)*.

Heine, K. (2011) *The Concept of Luxury Brands* (Berlin: Technische Universität Berlin, Department of Marketing).

Hockerts, K., and R. Wüstenhagen (2009) *Emerging Davids versus Greening Goliaths* (Frederiksberg, Denmark: CBS Center for Corporate Social Responsibility).

Ilari, A., and L. Zargani (2007) 'Italian Television Program Alleges Fashion Misconduct', *Women's Wear Daily*, 4 December 2007: 2.

Kapferer, J.N., and V. Basten (2010) *The Luxury Strategy: Break the Rules of Marketing to Build Luxury Brands* (London: Kogan Page).

Kleanthous, A. (2011) 'Simple the Best is no Longer Simple', *Raconteur on Sustainable Luxury*, July 2011: 3 (theraconteur.co.uk/category/sustainability/sustainable-luxury, accessed December 2012).

Markides, C., and P. Geroski (2005) *Fast Second: How Smart Companies Bypass Radical Innovation to Enter and Dominate Markets* (San Francisco: Jossey-Bass).

Mebratu, D. (1998) 'Sustainable and Sustainable Development: Historical and Conceptual Review', *Environmental Impact Assessment Review* 18.6: 493-520.

Meyerson, D.E., and M.A. Scully (1995) 'Tempered Radicals and the Politics of Ambivalence and Change', *Organization Science* 6.5: 585-600.

Monterrubio, C.L. (2008) *Los Tenangos, Mitos y Ritos Bordados: Arte Textil Hidalguense* (México: Conaculta).

Moore, B. (2011) 'Style Over Substance: Why Ethics Are Not in Fashion for Designer Labels', Ethical Consumer Research Association, www.ethicalconsumer.org/buyersguides/clothing/designerclothing.aspx, accessed December 2012.

Morgan, J. (2011) 'Leading by Nature', in J. Marshall, G. Coleman and P. Reason (eds.), *Leadership for Sustainability: An Action Research Approach* (Sheffield, UK: Greenleaf Publishing).

Mortelmans, D. (2005) 'Sign Values in Processes of Distinction: The Concept of Luxury', *Semiotica* 157.1/4: 497-520.

O'Malley, Ch. (2011) 'Lessons from the Entrepreneurial Path', in J. Marshall, G. Coleman and P. Reason (eds.), *Leadership for Sustainability: An Action Research Approach* (Sheffield, UK: Greenleaf Publishing).

PPR HOME (2011) 'PPR HOME . . . for the long run', PPR HOME, about.puma.com/wp-content/themes/aboutPUMA_theme/media/pdf/2011/en/PRESS_KIT_PPR_HOME.pdf, accessed 6 December 2013.

Saviano, R. (2007) *Gomorrah* (Barcelona: Randon House Mondadoni SA).

Schaltegger, S., and M. Wagner (2011) 'Sustainable Entrepreneurship and Sustainability Innovation: Categories and Interactions', *Business Strategy and the Environment* 20.4: 222-37.

Scheibel, S. (no date) *Ethical Luxury: Myth or Trend?* (Essay; London: London School of Economics and Political Science).

Schumpeter, J. (1934) *The Theory of Economic Development: An Inquiry into Profits, Capital, Credit, Interest, and the Business Cycle* (Cambridge, MA: Harvard University Press).

Thomas, D. (2007) *Deluxe: How Luxury Lost its Luster* (New York: Penguin Books).

Villiger, A., R. Wüstenhagen and A. Meyer (2000) *Jenseit der Öko-Nische* (Basel: Birkhäuser).

WCED (World Commission on Environment and Development) (1987) *Our Common Future* (Oxford, UK: Oxford University Press).

Weber, C. (2007) 'The Devil Sells Prada', *New York Times*, 26 August 2007 (www.nytimes.com/2007/08/26/books/review/Weber-t.html?adxnnl=1&adxnnlx=1374667433-b8wWiT9lWxPq+lu7FYYc5g, accessed June 2011).

1

Elvis & Kresse, UK

Kresse Wesling
Company founder and director

We can't beat nature. We can only try. We can cut old hoses until we can't unclench our gripping fingers, we can clean the hose until we can't stand up straight, we can skip every weekend and holiday for years but we won't beat nature. The harvest moon wins; the stillness and majesty of a quiet stand of old growth evergreens, the everyday differences of the sea, the gut flipping glimpse of a bear cub while hiking with friends, the hulking mass of the Rockies—they win.

The evolution of this particular entrepreneur starts with the eye-watering beauty of big nature. I knew very early on that I couldn't beat it; it just took me a while to work out how to join in.

An environmental entrepreneur

I had the great fortune to grow up in Western Canada at a time when kids could roam fairly freely, playing cops and robbers, making perfume from honeysuckles and lilacs. Everyone tells me about how precocious and dictatorial I was, two traits I have probably not lost, much to Elvis's dismay. Great family, great community, great state schooling, field trips to sewage treatment plants, skiing, skating, hockey, horse riding in the summers in the mountains. Running with my dad, going to the dump with my dad, picking berries with my grandmother and pickling, jamming and pieing with her, my mom, my sister. A lot of camping. A lot of lake swimming. I had no idea that Rundle Park, the big fields between my grandmother's and the North Saskatchewan River, were in fact a grassed over former landfill . . . maybe I got the waste bug from rolling down those hills?

I can safely skim through my teenage years; we moved a lot, I was over-stimulated and confused a lot of the time, but focused on school. I wanted to be everything from a Vet to the Prime Minister . . . so yeah, confused. More great schooling, at Li Po Chun United World College in Hong Kong and then back to Canada for a joint honours degree in East Asian Studies and Political Science . . . where I discovered that politics isn't really a science and definitely wasn't for me. But I learned how to digest a lot of information really quickly and this was the basis for a life-long study into everything that I find interesting, which mostly has to do with waste, nature and innovation.

I went back to Hong Kong after university, pretty much on a whim, and got my first proper job with a venture capital company. It was here, working for two years with an incredible woman, Amy Kong, that I got a taste for what I believe to be the few truly alluring and potentially redeeming features of business. If you can make some money from an idea, no one can tell you what to do, make you compromise or shut you down. This total freedom is why businesses have the potential to cut deep, scarring chasms or lift whole communities out of poverty and everything in between. Thank you, Amy!

Entrepreneurship is also the natural home for someone like me: excitable, ambitious, foolhardy, undauntable, conceptually creative—but I would be and have been unsuccessful in this space with the wrong partner. Elvis is my ideal match in every sense: focused, rational, relentless, funny and genuinely talented as a maker, a craftsperson. It is often said about our social enterprise that I am the social and he is the enterprise, but it isn't said enough that I have dreams that he is somehow able to realise. Thank you, Elvis!

I could give you a potted history of my other businesses but the reality is that they were either the right idea at the wrong time, the right idea but the wrong team or the wrong idea altogether. Moving on is always difficult but a stubborn entrepreneur will end up broke and alone so accepting and internalising a failure is an important skill. This becomes even more important in a succeeding business, where more is at stake. You have to continually assess progress and failures and change tack accordingly.

Once I had started down the business route, there really was no turning back and equally there was no way for me to think of business without thinking about it as a change agent. My personal goals are environmental, probably due to the sharp shock of moving back and forth between Canada and Hong Kong, Beijing and South China, so any business I have ever or would ever be associated with has the environment at its core. Money is the means; saving the planet is the end. And it is that clear cut; if you aren't fixing something, there is no point. If it's just about money then it's pointless. Some things are black and white.

Hose, beautiful hose

I moved to London in 2004. I followed Elvis; we'd met just over two years earlier in Hong Kong. It was a dream to be living in London, to run along the Thames and hear Big Ben chiming away, to be constantly, wonderfully lost. I saw as many waste transfer stations and industrial estates as I did museums and galleries, waste is always the best way to see what is wrong with a place. If I were a doctor I suppose I would focus on the intestines or the kidneys or the liver—the guts, the filters, the way we deal with inefficiencies, no matter how small. I never expected the UK to be as heavily reliant on landfill as it was; such a small space with so many people. There isn't land to spare. In the year I arrived over 100 million tonnes of waste was buried. And landfill is inexcusable, not just in a time of austerity; it is lazy, childish, uncivilised and disrespectful . . . The Earth hurtles through space, with no practical way of getting more of something or getting rid of anything else . . . this reality is so obvious, so undeniable, that the last 50+ years of forgetting to value raw materials really does mark out this era as being the least respectful of resources and the least aware of our utter dependence on this one Earth for all our lives.

But that is dark and deep and heavy, and not at all like our approach. We don't rail against the status quo and neither of us are stern campaigners. We aren't the only ones who feel that sometimes being green fails because it has mostly been marketed as worthy, and not fun. So it is not surprising that I first met the London Fire Brigade through a very worthy ISO14001 auditing course where I had a lot of fun chatting with firemen, particularly intrigued by one of their environmental issues. And what an issue it was: fire hoses, which can serve for up to 25 years, fighting fires and saving lives, must be decommissioned when they are too old or, more frequently, too damaged to repair. London has a whole team dedicated to patching and refurbishing but in the end some cuts are too deep, some holes are too large and shortening hoses to remove the damage isn't a solution when most hoses need to be over 20 metres long to do the job.

I didn't know what to do with the material, just that I would do something. Landfill was an indecent end for a heroic material. Although we didn't plan it, didn't know it at the time, the way we approached the hose has come to define our practice: tackling problems with solutions that deliver across many fronts.

Start with a problem. Fall in love with a problem. If you are fixing something there is a sense of purpose, which can push you through the difficult early days or years; there is also a greater potential for success. Solving something that no one else has been able to can make you unique, in demand. This works for the paradigms of both waste and luxury.

In our minds the solution then has to meet three criteria: it has to be sustainable, scalable and engaging.

Sustainability means both environmentally and socially sound *and* financially viable. If it is bad for the planet there is no point and if it is never going to be able to pay its own way then there is no future in it, no way to scale and no real chance to solve that particular problem. If we had to superheat the hose or dye it with toxic chemicals then it wouldn't be sustainable. If we had to sell our products below our cost prices then we would run out of steam. If we forced down the costs to a point where our craftspeople were tempted to lie about who makes the pieces or where they are made, then, again, it wouldn't be sustainable. You have to use your imagination and common sense; you have to value what you love. The planet isn't an added extra, it isn't a CSR programme, it is everything.

Scalability means that the solution in question has to be of equal magnitude to the problem. Tinkering is fine when you are trying to work out what to do; it's great for brainstorming and coming up with new concepts. But for us a solution is the goal, so we aren't prepared to tinker long term. We have to work out a way to deal with the whole thing, not the edges, not a portion, not some. All. Scalability also means that there has to be a way to grow without putting sustainability at risk.

Engageability[5] means fun, innovative, aspirational, alluring, multi-dimensional, conversation worthy. An engaging product isn't suitable

---

5 which I did have to look up, as it doesn't quite sound like a real word to me, but does appear on various online dictionaries in exactly the way I want to use it . . .

for a one-night-stand; it is marriage material. We are not talking about something you like, but something you love, something you are committed to. For Elvis and I the belts have to be designed to stay on your favourite jeans, outlast them, and then be transferred to a new pair when your jeans wear out. For too long the green movement has been a bit depressing. But the guilt has to go, we have to sell these ideas, they have to be better, more compelling, more wonderful than the less green, less ethical alternatives. Marketing is a positive, upbeat, affirmational pursuit, so why change it? Use it! Make something so outstanding, so awesome and so inspiring that it deserves the hype. This isn't a case of 'if you can't beat them, join them', it is definitely, absolutely and entirely a case of 'this is the absolute coolest thing we can do, we already beat them, they're just going to have to join us'. In this regard, engageability is entwined with scalability. If we want to foster system change—the complete realignment of consumption—then we aren't talking about our journey anymore; this is going to have to be one heck of a convoy.

From shed to factory, waste to luxury

So let's rewind, back to 'I didn't know what to do with the hose, just that I would do something'. How did we do it, how did we get here, how did a pile of hose become a brand, a business, a powerful way to prove the inherent value in a seemingly useless pile of rubbish? How did we go from decommissioned hoses to luxury handbags? The short answer is, 'not how we thought we would'. This is definitely a question we can only answer retrospectively. It is relatively easy to look back at the path we took, but when we were on it, when we were travelling, there was no path to follow.

Our first focus was the hose itself, its rich lustrous red, its strength, and its water resistance. We were sharing the house of a dear friend, Tom. Tom and Elvis were building a shed in the back garden for our bikes. Our first ever trial with the hose was as roof tiles for the shed, cut into flat rectangles and applied like clay tiles, slates or cedar shakes . . . This was before we knew how to edge the hose, so the tiles were flattened, but still round, still hose-like. It was pretty, but heavy. Ultimately, as appealing as roofing was as a solution, it didn't fit the problem. There isn't enough hose waste, globally, annually, to have a sustainable roofing company. And, as we discovered later, the hose doesn't love to live permanently in the sun; it browns, it ages and it weathers faster than a roof should. Back to the drawing board . . . and there were many drawing boards . . . We made many prototypes in those first years that would have taken us in completely different directions but none seemed to suit the hose, none would solve the problem. And then came the first belt.

Elvis had one belt, a classic he likely inherited from his father, thick brown leather with a brass West End buckle. Its long life and a few years in Hong Kong's humidity had taken their toll and cracks that had been growing finally led to a split. The belt was dead but the buckle was still alive and kicking. Elvis cut a length of hose to replace the leather last, and the timing could not have been better. While he was fixing it to the buckle I received a call from the team working on merchandise for London's Live Earth concert. They needed something green, apropos of the event, and in my own impulsive style I promised to deliver 1,000 belts. The trial by fire began, a night of furious hose-cutting ensued and we woke with claw-like hands, ruined by the effort of cutting perfectly straight lengths with house scissors . . . 1,000 would be impossible. We called back and dropped the commitment to 500 and then went out to find a suitable cutting tool. Our first rotary cutter, at £39.99, constitutes the only capital investment we ever made that wasn't financed by sales. That month, when we developed our first technique for cleaning hose—moving quickly from the bathtub to scrubbing with an abrasive, industrial broom—was definitely do or die. We had to source and brand buckles, we had to work out how to edge and finish the hose, we had to beg and borrow space to work and clean (mostly from Elvis's now long-suffering family), and we did all of this while keeping existing jobs.

The belts sold well; we used the proceeds to buy a sewing machine. Elvis learned to sew. We started making more belts and set up a website, we also worked with the now extinct London Fire Brigade online store to sell belts branded for the LFB. We knew we couldn't live by belts alone and started thinking about how to expand the range—then I came across a key piece of research, one of the major leather luxury brands uses as much leather, annually, as there is hose . . . so we had an appropriate solution . . . we just needed (and still need) to become a major luxury brand . . .

Our first problem was manufacturing. We needed a partner with skilled craftspeople that could work with our material and our designs. Elvis started a sketchbook that we still have, where we focused on classic pieces, ones that sell and sell, which are part of the permanent collections you see in high-end department stores across the world. Totes, washbags, wallets, cardholders, messengers . . . Elvis re-imagined these classics with both the qualities and constraints of the hose foremost in his mind. Then we loaded ourselves up with hose and went to see the best manufacturers we could find in the UK. In most cases we didn't get further than a phone call:

> 'Hi, we are looking to order a small run of products made from redundant fire hose, which we will supply, cleaned and ready to go.'

> 'We only work with leather.'

> 'We only produce for our own brand.'

> 'We are a *premium manufacturer.*'

We couldn't find a British manufacturer that wanted our business; perhaps we were unlucky in that the recession hadn't taken hold, they didn't need us. So we started moving beyond the UK, into Spain, Italy, France, Portugal . . . the answers were the same.

We thought it might just be the hose, it looked too much like hose—it was still coiled up and carried in slung over one of our shoulders. Elvis went back to the sewing machine. We needed to prove our pieces could be made. So Elvis made them—but it would never do to make one bag a week, at that rate we would need to charge a small fortune for them. We went back to all the factories with our now finished, however rudimentary, pieces. This time some of them bit, but unused to the material as they were the results weren't great, the costs spiralled and in the end most still pulled out because 'it just isn't leather'.

Then Elvis went to Romania, and we met a small, family-run factory that was willing to take a chance. They had three crucial qualities: a gap in their production schedule, a serious pedigree of production for major luxury brands, and they believed like we did, that the hose deserved to be treasured, that it wasn't a leather substitute but a thing of beauty in its own right. We sampled four designs, and brought them back to the UK to work out a plan. The minimum order was for 800 pieces across the four styles. Our burgeoning belt business was doing well but we hadn't sold enough to finance this production run quite yet, so while we cleaned, prepared and shipped pallets of material to Romania, I went all over London, introducing our original Classic Tote to anyone and everyone and started selling them—pre-selling at a 30% discount—and promising delivery in a few months time. Those miraculous first customers, heaven-sent chance takers, were how we got that first run off the ground, almost a year after we made the Live Earth belts.

When we started collecting the hoses I made a promise to our contacts at the London Fire Brigade, that we would share 50% of the profits with the Fire Fighters Charity (FFC). I am sure they never thought a donation would ever materialise, but when we ran through our accounts at the end of that first year there was something left. We hadn't made a profit, not really, we hadn't paid ourselves, and our accountant later told us that we had actually made a loss, but a promise is a promise. Instead of dividing the meagre remains, we sent that full amount, 134 precious pounds, to the FFC. Thankfully, donations have been increasing year on year and have all gone out with our accountant's approval.

We get asked a lot about this commitment, why we do it, why we have extended it across all the materials we reclaim. It started as a gesture of goodwill; they were sharing their hose with us, we should share our proceeds back with them. But there are so many more reasons. We will always be asked this question, but we now find ourselves asking other companies why they don't share, why they aren't generous with their stakeholders. Collecting the hose saves the brigades money (no landfill charges); this saving and the donations have helped us to build and solidify strong relationships with our key raw material suppliers. Giving in this way helped us to build a community around our small brand; there are 66,000 fire service personnel in the UK and both the brigades and the FFC are incredible at telling our story to this key group of ambassadors. Our customers love this story too; by supporting us they participate in the giving; not only are we delivering a beautiful, hand-crafted piece, we are delivering the powerful narrative of the life-saving hoses and giving back to the fire service personnel who save our lives. Writing donation cheques when we have finished the annual accounts has become a day of celebration for us. It is one of the highlights of the year.

There has never been a pattern to our days, we work out what needs to happen each week or each day based on orders coming in or people we need to meet. All activity is coordinated around two major themes: constant improvement and momentum.

Constant improvement

One of the things that must make life incredibly difficult for Elvis, other than me, is that he is always certain he can do better. In almost 12 years I don't think he has ever shrugged, said 'oh well', 'whatever', 'I did my best', or anything even remotely like that. The products have to be outstanding, have to impress him, or we aren't doing right by the hose. As his techniques and knowledge have increased, the quality has been improving, and although improvements are now incremental as opposed to overwhelming, they are still an important driver. And improvement doesn't end with product—it only starts there. We are now on our fourth website; the first three were built entirely by Elvis, the latest was a collaboration between Elvis and a professional team, but I know it will not remain static. The images will forever be a work in progress. The packaging is light years ahead of where it was, even 12 months ago.

Although it wasn't a product, per se, Elvis's most incredible achievement was our first home. We bought the most awful flat with the most incredible potential and rebuilt it virtually entirely with materials we reclaimed or found second-hand. Again, when it was complete, we both felt that we needed to sell it, in order to by a factory, in order to take on a new challenge. It is a testament to the quality of the finish that the final negotiations on the sale were for the purchase of all the handmade furniture, curtains, shutters and cabinetry. I can't wait to see what can be done at the new site—which is over five times larger than the flat.

Elvis is also always improving our logistics and production, and everything about how the business operates. He streamlines, he tweaks . . . perhaps this is down to his sailing. He is a qualified ocean master yachtsman, a celestial navigator. He loves lowering shipping costs, or redesigning packaging, making it easier to assemble. He is always thinking about how, why and where we do things. When a major luxury brand swooped into our factory in Romania and bought up all of its capacity for two years, we should have taken it as a compliment . . . they were after the quality that we demanded. It could have been a disaster, we could have lost our ability to manufacture, but Elvis took this as yet another opportunity to get better, and has established our own dedicated factory in Turkey. Here it will be easier to innovate, and take the products to even greater levels.

Momentum

Constant improvement is inward looking and largely managed by Elvis; momentum is outward looking, and very much my domain. I know, in the end, if the business fails, it will not be down to the products, it will be down to lack of sales, growth, strategic direction … it will be down to me. Live Earth was an early success but we have never rested, we are constantly pursuing new materials (and consequently charities), retail partners, PR opportunities, collaborations and projects well beyond our comfort zone. There was no audience for fire hose handbags in the UK, we had to build one: knocking on loads of doors to find our first stockists, running our own PR and networking like there is no tomorrow. In many ways, this is an easy job. I love the search for new waste and I love meeting people. I can imagine a time when the business is big enough that I may only have two roles, waste hunter and brand ambassador.

I didn't and still don't have an elevator pitch, I have an everywhere pitch, and it is easy, this is what I love to do, what else would I talk about? The role of our family, friends, their contacts and their contacts' contacts cannot be understated. Our story is designed to be shared, it is compelling, funny, genuine and there are very few people that we have met who are not keen to pass the story on. Most people go beyond that, most love to help out. Reaching out and giving back creates an incredible, very rideable wave. In our very early days someone mentioned a call for social enterprise ambassadors, and when we were just working on our first bags the Cabinet Office appointed me. This was an amazing opportunity to tell our story, to inspire more social entrepreneurship, to build a network among the best social entrepreneurs in the country. We entered many business plan awards, and won. Success and recognition breed, build and multiply.

We were constantly meeting press. The more press we had, the more we sold online, the easier it was to find new stockists, the easier it was to find collaborators, the easier it was to take on more challenges. As these things became easier we started to develop a profile, got asked to speak more, and got to meet yet more press. I think the media has an unbelievably crucial role; they are the ones who can question, verify, attest, highlight, dig . . . They ask the difficult questions; they push us forward. I know a lot of people thought we were crazy until we made it into the *Sunday Times*. There was no more talk of crazy after 2009 when our West End belt was the star red item in an all-white shoot in US Vogue, where Cameron Diaz was wearing our belt over a Phillip Lim dress. We have had a few journalists come to stay, and in our new home/factory we hope to have many more guests.

Beyond fire hose

Bizarre heading . . . I am not sure we will ever be beyond hose. By 2010 we were able to successfully reclaim and re-engineer all of London's hose and are expanding collection across the country, so we are progressing with our mission, but it is not yet complete. We may not complete it, even if we grow to take all the world's hoses we would still have to maintain that scale. This doesn't really worry me though, there is sustained appetite for other classics; Louis Vuitton has been selling the brown, coated, monogrammed bags since 1959.[6] Where there is a will, there is a way! But the hose has never been our whole story. Even in the very beginning we refused to work with traditional packaging, making our own instead, from other locally reclaimed materials. The linings, gift cards, business cards, even our first home, all are/were designed with reclaimed materials.

So now we look to new wastes and new challenges, ways to grow the brand without compromising our core principles, ways to expand the practice. Crucial to this has been finding a more permanent

6 Johnston, R. (2012) 'King Louis', *GQ*, 12 July 2012 (www.gq-magazine. co.uk/style/articles/2012-07/12/louis-vuitton-history-of-luxury-label-and-outlets-shops-bags-shoes, accessed 10 December 2013).

home, both for our workshop and us. We have moved more than five times since 2007, starting with a makeshift belt production line in our bedroom. From there we progressed to a rented garage, our first small workshop and then two larger workshops . . . but we wanted something we could reclaim, own, grow into . . . We found Tonge Mill in early 2013 and moved in June. It is a 200-year-old water mill that requires complete restoration and internal development. It is perfect. From Tonge we have already launched our first ever collaboration with a major designer, Bill Amberg, and we have also launched our first ever non-hose collection, a new material challenge that currently results in over 200 tonnes of valuable textile waste to landfill in the UK each year.

My grandmother, my hero, grew up in a different time, a wasteless one. Her bedtime stories were about how to store cabbage through the winter. Her gifts were quilts made from scraps of worn-out clothing. Transforming perceptions of this ethic from hardship and necessity into the new decadence, the new luxury, is, I suppose, the work of our business, possibly the work of our lifetime. We are small but ambitious, there is no reason to think that we can't change the industry. We can be a part of developing an economy without waste, where materials all continue to move, create value and solve problems. And the only way for us to do this is to be great. Our pieces must be treasures in order to be treasured. Our story has to be worth re-telling. We have to inspire. I think the luxury industry inspires already, but we want it to inspire a love for the environment, respect for resources. We want it to inspire giving.

In 2012 we were named one of Walpole's Brands of Tomorrow. At the launch party we were introduced by programme chair, John Ayton, as 'the future of luxury'. This is what we have to live up to, just this and big nature . . .

2

The IOU Project, Spain
Turning supply chains into prosperity chains

Kavita Parmar
Company founder and director

I am a self-taught designer and a serial entrepreneur. I was born in India and educated in India and England. At the age of 18, while attending university, I started my own studio working as a freelance designer for various international clothing brands. So I spent most of my adult life working in the fashion industry and have had the fortune to live and work in many parts of the world: India, Singapore, London, Hong Kong, San Francisco, New York to name a few, and now Madrid.

The IOU Project was born out of my frustration as a designer with the current fashion system. All about *faster* and *cheaper*, it has become a race to the bottom and does not nurture *big design* (not just making things pretty but truly designing the ecosystem around the production to make it sustainable), or value provenance, excellent craftsmanship or artisanship.

I don't believe sustainable and responsible fashion to be a trend but a real need for our times. Quality and authenticity were the first victims of keeping up with the latest short-lived trend and this voracious cycle of consumption we were feeding into. No one today is unaware of the scarcity of resources we face, the damage to the environment or the living conditions endured by a large part of the world's population, just so that a few of us can consume irresponsibly.

This is too high a price and without any doubt unsustainable.

I love my work and was no longer happy doing it, so I decided to stop complaining and do something about it. Focusing on what was most important to me as a designer, the artisan who helped me make my designs a reality and the customer who bought them, in 2010 my husband and partner Iñigo Puente and I started working on the idea as a small experiment.

Iñigo is an engineer from MIT and has always had the belief that with the current technology we had the tools to truly disrupt the fashion industry. In the beginning it seemed like a Herculean task. I wanted to make each piece unique and traceable back to the artisans who made it to give them authorship and pride. It took us over a year to just get the first part right and we were lucky enough to get a few friends involved who were very interested in the idea. We knew that there was a small part of the audience that cared about the ideas of traceability and transparency but we wanted to reach out to a larger audience.

I have worked in many projects with artisan communities in my career to varying success. When it is done for a very reduced elite customer base, if the product is good, yes, you sell out and if the story is powerful you get a lot of press but the number of people impacted are not enough to make real change happen.

I was obsessed with the idea of addressing a larger market; that you could buy a piece at a reasonable price point and that it was truly unique felt like important sales arguments.

I wanted the first collection to be around an authentic story and what could be more authentic than Gandhi's non-violent revolution? He inspired millions of Indians to buy local, handmade fabrics to fight against the cheaper machine-made imports from imperialistic 19th-century England to give back work to the local craftsman.

So we worked on the first collection with handloom weavers from Tamil Nadu. The cooperative societies we work with were founded in 1927 inspired by Mahatma Gandhi, making them a perfect fit.

The weavers made 8 m of unique patterns, as that was the size of the warp on their looms. This makes it very difficult for them to work with mass-market clothing brands that need large quantities of exactly the same pattern to get economies of scale. No weaver wants to repeat the same pattern over and over again. It is monotonous and plain boring and of course ends up having them compete against machine-made fabrics, which is an impossible fight.

But this is exactly what made them very appealing to us, so we decided to use their perceived weakness as our strength. There are over 250,000 handloom weavers in the greater area of Tamil Nadu so variety with scale was not a problem.

We wanted to produce clothing with the best makers and Europe with its artisanal tradition was right at hand. Living in Europe for the last 12 years, it has been disheartening to see how difficult it is for small, high-quality producers to survive against the **fast fashion** onslaught.

I have worked with artisan producers in Europe and India for most of my career so it made perfect sense to combine and foster these relationships between artisans in India and in Europe. Both were suffering and finding a solution where they could work together to create a high-quality product for the final consumer seemed like the perfect solution.

But working with the artisan factories in Europe was another matter. Making each piece unique meant changing the way things were done at the factory floor level.

In the last 20 years the focus of all factories and ateliers has been to increase productivity, as they had to compete with global sourcing. We had to go back to how things were made before when a very small, reduced group made the entire piece. This gave us better quality and traceability. What was magical was that it also gave back authorship and brought back pride to the artisan.

Creating the on line and off line traceability system was one of the most challenging tasks but it has also been the most rewarding. Making people aware of each other in the chain has been one of the true successes of the project, something that I cannot describe on a balance sheet but have witnessed repeatedly in the proud smiles of the artisans when they see the *Prosperity Chain* on the web.

Our focus is on value and quality. There is a huge imbalance in people's perception of value. The industry has convinced the consumer to accept low quality for a cheaper price point and turned everything into a disposable product. Why then are we shocked when stories of inhuman labour conditions are revealed every other day? We as consumers have voted for that by buying into this irresponsible consumption pattern.

Using transparency and traceability we aim to turn the supply chain into what we call a **prosperity chain**. We buy from the weavers and the artisans at the fair price they ask and we work on low mark-ups compared with the normal industry standards to ensure that the final price is competitive.

Each IOWEYOU Madras piece is unique and has an IOU code (QR code) that takes you to its story simply by scanning it with a smartphone or just entering the number on our website. On the site you can see the weaver who hand wove that particular fabric in India and then the artisan in Europe who turned that fabric into a beautifully handcrafted piece. We encourage the customer to take their picture and upload it to complete the story so that the weaver in India and the artisan in Europe can also see who bought that piece.

That simple gesture of acknowledgment gives them a huge sense of pride. Most of us know so little about how and who makes the things we use daily, by putting a face to that object you **de-commoditise** it, make it human and turn it into something to cherish, we hope.

No one really believed that we could make it happen and most people said the consumer doesn't really care about these ideas.

But I have good news, the consumer does care and the proof is in the pudding. Being a self-funded start up and this being a *new idea* that took a lot of time and resources to develop, when we went live we had no money left for marketing or PR.

But people spread the word like wildfire. We continue to receive emails from people around the globe who love the idea and want to support us.

Also we added the very consumer engaging **trunk show host** feature. Since as a company we were being disruptive with the current supply chain, why not take that one step further and do the same experiment with distribution of the brand. On our website people who are truly interested in the project can have their own **trunk show**. It is like having your own virtual IOWEYOU store. You apply to become a trunk show host and once you are set up (all you need is a Facebook and PayPal account) you get to choose your favourite pieces, which are tagged with your name. You blog, tweet, post and/or email your social circle and make 20% of the price of each item sold through you. You can keep that money, give it as a discount to your followers or pay it back to the weaver. The decision is yours. It's a great way to share your style and your beliefs.

We have been in Beta with this app and the reaction has been incredible.

A lot of the buzz generated around the IOU Project has come from these initial trunk show hosts. We have over 300 and they are from all around the globe and are pretty committed folk. We are working on adding more products and more artisans to the IOU Project. Many artisan communities from around the globe have contacted us and we are currently in development with one community in Scotland and others in Mexico and Tibet. The dream is of creating a working

Wikipedia of artisan communities around the globe to help preserve these rich traditions.

We are shipping worldwide. I am proud to say that in the first year of being online we had shipped to over 30 countries. But I must highlight that the US is our biggest market.

The IOU Project also offers partner retailers and other brands the possibility of using our platform and our **MAAP** (mass aggregated artisan produced) system to produce their designs. We are in talks with leading brands and retailers in the industry who are very excited about using our **Prosperity Chain** to create product for their customer base.

It has been an exciting 2 years. The IOU Project has received a lot of industry recognition, awards such as, the 2012 Luxury Briefing Award for Innovation of the Year in London; 2012 SOURCE Awards by Ethical Fashion Forum London; Best Performance in Sustainable Luxury in Latin America Award 2012 in Buenos Aires; 2012 New York City NY Venture Fellows program; and 2013 Unreasonable at Sea program.

I have been invited to speak on sustainability in fashion and new emerging trends at the United Nations Leaders program in Torino, Italy, TEDx Barcelona, TEDx Big Apple in New York, TEDx Navigli, Beyond Fashion Berlin, Pechacucha in Spain, Instituto Cervantes in New Delhi, Fonart in Mexico, Instituto Rio de Moda in Rio de Janeiro, SxSW Eco in Austin USA and many universities and conferences. Besides, there is a lot more cooking in the pot for the future.

The idea was born out of the spirit of collaboration and the belief that human progress depends on our ability to do so. Real collaboration can only happen when there is true transparency and traceability for everyone involved.

I believe the future of responsible consumption and responsible production is about making everyone who buys and sells more aware of each other. Knowing the people behind the product or putting a face to the final customer impacts people on both sides, making them more conscious of how they consume and how they produce. That is a huge step in the right direction. The problems that we face as humanity today are not trivial and there are no easy solutions but taking individual responsibility and having mutual respect is a great place to start.

I am also very grateful to all the people, and there have been many, who have helped us make this a reality, given us a chance to make change happen and to be able to tell my children a good story about this incredible journey.

3

Aïny Savoirs des Peuples, France

Daniel Joutard
Company founder and director

The foundation of Aïny

Aïny is both a young and an old company; young, because we launched the brand in 2009, and old, because it was conceived after a long development process. It is rooted in the community work I did in the late 1990s in Ecuador, in communities related to the peasant and indigenous movement. I was just a grad from a business administration school in Paris and wanted to discover South America off the beaten track. I went to work in small villages to give advice to peasant organisations and help them increase their production added value and reap more benefits from their work. Back then, my biggest concern was where I would go out on Saturday night, but in Ecuador I was spending time with people who struggled for their economic and cultural survival. I worked with people that gave life a very profound meaning. Moreover, these people looked at the world in a very 'magical' manner, since for them everything—from rivers to trees and hills—had a soul, a spirit . . . And when you see the world through those eyes, you respect it a lot more and find it much more poetical.

I also met a young female healer who told me about the power of plants and the magic in this world. As I was every inch a Frenchman with diplomas from important schools, I knew that the world was ruled by rationality and science, that magic and plants were a nice folklore, or worse, a fraud, but in any case, not a serious matter. But since that was her entire life, she shut herself off and did not talk about that for many years.

Then, I went back to France and worked as a consultant for large corporations, but I always came back to Ecuador and South America, to the Andes, to the Amazonian region, to these remote communities I liked so much. And when I got sick or twisted my foot, as there was no Western medicine to heal me, I was taken to the Ecuadorian healer or to the village wise men, and it worked. Maybe I was not that open-minded back then, but I was rational, so if it worked, then there must be something in it. And this is how I got into the plants that healers used in their magical rites and to heal.

And this has nothing to do with chance; in most cases, these plants have a strong biological activity—what we call science, chemistry or biology, they call magic and energy, but we mean the same thing.

After six years as a consultant in France, I decided to go back to the countryside and work with peasants and natives and took off to Peru, but this time in small microcredit fund management. Once again, I become immersed in this magical world and, when I was back in France, it hit me that I wanted to work with sacred plants, though I didn't know how.

In 2006, I contacted Jean Claude Le Joliff, former R&D director at Chanel. He agreed to see me and gave me 30 minutes to speak. At the end, we spent the entire afternoon and he ended up offering his services for free. He found my story interesting and wanted to help.

I already had my scientific director and a major consultant for the company strategy.

Since I was interested in some seeds, and had people in Peru and Ecuador who knew how to harvest them, we began our research. We hired a chemical engineer and created our own lab. We worked for three years to transform these seeds into active cosmetic extracts and these, in turn, into unique sensory creams.

In 2008, although there was still a long way to go in product development, we made a presentation at the most important International Cosmetic Fair in France (Beyond Beauty), and received the jury's special award. A year later, we returned to the tradeshow and, again, we were awarded for best natural and organic brand. In September 2009, the products were on sale.

Our values

What makes the value of top luxury brand products? What justifies the high price of a Hermès bag or a Chanel dress?

These brands will explain that it takes a lot of time to manufacture these products, that they will require the hands of a highly skilled craftsman, and that, besides, as it will be impossible to make many of them, supply will be low . . . Time-intensive, the hand of man, limited quantity, and quality mean luxury . . .

The plants used by healers in their rituals and their traditional knowledge are a way of true luxury. And we need these plants. Of course, a world-class scientific team is essential—but not enough—to create an outstanding cosmetic. You need plants with a strong biological activity, and an inspirational story.

You need a shaman or healer who has learned about plants from a very young age and will have a very tough learning process that will take many years, and who will point out to you certain facts about a plant and its uses . . . You need expert hands to crop the seeds or barks at the right time of the year and, even, at the right hour of the day, when the plant is at the peak of its activity. Plants need time to grow with no chemical aids, fertilisers or pesticides. For all those factors, we end up getting a limited quantity of top quality plants . . .

The hand of man, time, limited quantity . . . the characteristics of luxury that call for just the same respect you pay to craftsmen of top brands.

In Aïny, we are always grateful to and respectful of those people who share their knowledge with us, and also we owe them.

Part of this respect is to assimilate this wisdom and magic as part of our production development process. So, each of our products is tied to a magical chant (Icaros) drawn by a Peruvian shaman inside our cases.

To believe in magic does not mean to leave science aside. We are a hybrid company with roots in France, the country of cosmetic science. And though our scientific director Jean Claude—one of the leading experts in French cosmetics and a huge iconoclast—recommended that we should focus on magic, leaving science aside, I decided to turn science into a major pillar of our values, together with magic, instead of opposing them.

Our obsession is to have the best product possible, and science always helps improve quality and efficacy. It helps us constantly innovate in active principles and find new textures. Aïny has just discovered ways to create natural emulsions without heating the ingredients, which helps prevent breakdown of active components and saves carbon dioxide emissions. We are the first company to do this in France, and this wouldn't have been possible without our scientific team's three years of research.

Moreover, respect means accepting that indigenous communities— the people our company works with—give their feedback on our work and share the company's success and progress. So, every three years we negotiate agreements with the organisations that represent them. During these negotiations, we agree on the plants that we are allowed to study. Since we work with sacred plants, some of them may have too deep a symbolic meaning to allow for cosmetics use. We give back part of our profits to their organisation (4% of sales as per the current agreements) to be able to use their knowledge. These funds are used for biodiversity conservation projects, and to preserve their wisdom.

Moreover, in these agreements we undertake not to apply for plant-related patents. We believe it would be unfair to apply for patents, because of the invaluable contribution of these indigenous peoples to plant knowledge. If they are taken out in a clever way, these patents may restrict the use of the plant to the patent holder. Just like luxury brands defend their creations by attacking fake manufacturers, we find it unfair to patent a plant that was discovered and worked by indigenous peoples.

In fact, in order to avoid this patent registration, we publish part of our research in international journals to produce written evidence on this knowledge and wisdom. A patent assumes an innovation that is no longer so once our research is published.

The contribution of shamans and indigenous communities

Aïny was created with the inspiration, inputs and contributions of many indigenous people and communities of South America.

The Ecuadorian healer that I met many years ago played a starring role in Aïny. She opened the door to understanding what I could not understand, and taught me that listening comes before making any statement. She was present in all the key moments of Aïny, though always keeping a distance.

She gave us the company name. In *Quechua* language (or *Kichua* in Ecuador), Aïny can have several meanings. 'Ayni' means 'I help you today, you will help me tomorrow', which is a mainstay of the native communities of the Andes. It reminds us that we have to give back to those who contribute to Aïny's venture. In turn, in Quechua from Ancash (Peru), 'Hainy' means 'spirit of the living beings'. And we were lucky, since Aïny also means 'I love you' in Chinese and 'my eye' in Arabic.

Moreover, we launched a very ambitious venture with her. For the first time, we decided to bring these indigenous communities' body techniques (massages, vapour baths, etc.) closer to a broader audience. When we talk about massages, we always think of Asia. Even Latin American hotels offer Thai, Indian or Japanese massages, without knowing that a few miles away there are traditional therapists that master amazing techniques. For instance, I found healers specialised in beauty that had some sort of 'traditional beauty parlour' where they prepared creams, ointments and traditional vapour baths. I found a golden-hand bonesetter with very original and innovative techniques that relieve stress in a second with a quick massage on the spine and the head using the thumbs.

So, for a full month, she and a masseuse from the company got together to create body and face rituals, which combine Andean and Amazonian traditional techniques with Western massage and face care methods. The novelty and quality of this creation were widely recognised and discussed by French and international journalists. Nowadays, these massages are offered in the most exclusive hotels of the Orient Express chain in Peru or on luxury cruise ships.

We spent a lot of time with the Ashaninkas from Peru and their representatives from an organisation called CECONSEC (Central de las comunidades nativas de la selva central de Peru, Organisation of Native Communities of the Peruvian Central Amazonia). The Ashaninka is the biggest indigenous cultural group of the Peruvian jungle, gathering more than 40,000 people. They are located in the centre of the Peruvian Amazonia and expand beyond the border with Brazil. This community is very proud of traditions, and they are a people of warriors who were at the forefront during the violent years of the 1980s and 1990s. They are also a community of shamans and healers, called the Shiripiaris, who use plants and tobacco to heal. I found many fascinating traditions in these communities. For example, one of the plants we use is the *Sacha Inchi*. It is a climbing plant with a green, star-shaped fruit. Its seed has a sort of almond that provides a very appealing oil for cosmetics since it has the highest content of Omega 3 (50%), 6 (37%), and 9 (9%) oils. Omega 3 has interesting properties as it reduces skin puffiness, which may be one of the reasons for early ageing. Omega 6 and 9 oils emulate skin components and enable the repair and strengthening of its natural barrier capacity.[7] But this is common knowledge for Ashaninka grandmothers, who use this plant in beauty rituals. Native communities also produce cosmetics and, in this case, women prepare anti-age facials, by manually extracting the oil from the seed and mixing it with yuca flour or flour from the same seed.

Some French companies registered patents on the *Sacha Inchi*, which copied this knowledge. The company made an alliance among CECONSEC, an organisation representing approximately 20,000 Ashaninkas, the State of Peru, by means of the National Commission to Fight against Biopiracy (Comisión Nacional de Lucha contra la Biopiratería) and a group of French NGOs, to mount a 3-year campaign which was eventually successful. They forced companies to give up these patents after a 3-year media campaign in France.

Also in Peru, the company developed many relationships with Quechuan healers and shamans from the Cusco region. A biologist, professor at the University of Peru and expert in Andean medicine helped our company better understand the plants of the region, especially the *Molle* tree, which we use to make the essence of scents and that is native to the Andes. This tree has so many medicinal uses that it is called the 'tree of life' by native peasants. Among others, it is used in vapour baths to treat 'magical melancholy'. Some Brazilian researchers confirmed in a lab test the anti-depressant effect of its

7 Rousseau Aïny, C., and J.C. Le Joliff (2009) 'Sacha Inchi Oil and Ungurahua Oil: A New Lease on Life for Omegas in Cosmetics', *Household and Personal Care Today* 1: 6-8.

leaf extract, verifying, once again, the connection between magic and science.[8]

We also developed many relationships with the Achuar community. The Achuar community lives in the jungle of Ecuador and Peru. It is one of the best organised native communities that I came across during my trips. They keep their traditional culture but take the best parts of Western culture. In their councils, they can discuss the situation of a shaman who is to blame for damaging the crops in a community and review the accounting of the aviation company that they manage or the development plans for the luxury eco-lodge that they manage in their territory.

With them, and together with a local NGO, we began working with the *Ungurahui* oil—a wild palm tree of the Upper Amazonia. This tree bears a fruit with high concentration of Omega 9 that repairs the skin and is perfect for dry or aged skins.[9] For many Amazonian peoples, the *Ungurahui* is a protective tree; the Huaoranis, for example, use it for strength in combat. We also get to know the *Guayusa*, a plant with very high caffeine content and antioxidant polyphenols. The Achuar community uses it in healing ceremonies or to have visions before going hunting, or even before going to war (overconsumption of caffeine may cause a narcotic effect). Caffeine is a very interesting active ingredient in the cosmetics industry, since it helps break up fat and stimulates blood micro-circulation. It is perfect as an anti-ageing eye corrector, reducing bags and rings under the eyes or in weight management products. Polyphenols are antioxidants that help fight the traces of time, and they are excellent for anti-wrinkle creams.

8   Machado, D.G., M.P. Kaster, R.W. Binfaré, M. Dias, A.R. Santos, M.G. Pizzolatti, I.M. Brighente, A.L. Rodrigues (2007) 'Antidepressant-like Effect of the Extract from Leaves of Schinus molle L. in Mice: Evidence for the Involvement of the Monoaminergic System', *Progress in Neuro-Psychopharmacology and Biological Psychiatry, 30 March 2007*.

9   Rousseau Aïny, C., and J.C. Le Joliff (2009) 'Sacha Inchi Oil and Ungurahua Oil: A New Lease on Life for Omegas in Cosmetics', *Household and Personal Care Today* 1: 6-8.

We had an agreement with the NAE, which is the Spanish acronym for the organisation Achuar Nationality of Ecuador, but need to renew it and make the most out of it. The relationships with the Achuars are complicated because of the distance and isolation. The Achuar communities are very isolated and not very connected to the rest of the world.

The innovation

Aïny combines the best of traditional sciences and Western biology. Our scientific team is led by Jean Claude Le Joliff, who created Chanel labs in the 1970s, and held the R&D director position until the early 2000s.

Jean Claude encouraged us to have our own cosmetic research lab, which is very unusual for a brand like ours. Only top brands own their labs. Most other brands subcontract product development, and focus all their efforts on marketing and communication. We go for innovation and the highest possible quality. This calls for controlling product creation, mostly since we use organic formulation techniques which are handled by few people. So we created a lab in downtown Paris made up of a team of chemists, biologists and pharmacologists who work on extracts and creams.

From seeds or barks, we must create a product with the best possible texture and efficacy. This requires several steps and, while we are guided by traditional knowledge, we always have a long way to go which may take as long as three years. We study the best ways to extract active components in order to ensure optimal efficacy and respect for the plants and the environment. External scientific studies help us check the absolute innocuousness and efficacy of the extract. Then, we formulate the extract into the most suitable cream. Once again, we check finished product innocuousness using scientific tests. Throughout this process, we never test our products on animals, but we use alternative testing methods (which use skin from plastic surgery). We only launch products into the market once this long process is completed. As green formulation is constantly evolving, we change our formulas to make sure that they include the best available technology.

We also spend a great deal of time researching into cold emulsion formulation techniques. Cold formulation means to create cosmetics without heating the ingredients. To manufacture natural and organic cosmetics, many times it's necessary to heat the ingredients to allow mixing. For the first time in France and Europe, we discovered at least one way to develop cosmetic emulsions (mix of oils and water) without heating the ingredients. This helps preserve even more the efficacy of active components, in addition to reducing CO_2 emissions during manufacture. In 2012, we launched the first cold-formulated serum based on *Guayusa* polyphenols. Our entire product range will gradually migrate to this technology.

Our innovative capacity in cosmetic technology is gaining recognition in France and beyond. In 2011, we received Young Innovative Company Status granted by the French administration, and we also won the responsible technological innovation award of Paris in 2012.

Business model

You have to be mad to create a cosmetics company in France.

It's the most competitive market in the world, with giant local players and foreign players willing to come in and compete to earn the legitimacy granted by this country's history.

When I realised this, it was too late and I had no choice but to move forward. Although I was proud of it, the company's seed capital got a laugh from the directors of brands that I came across at first. I was trying to understand what I was getting into, and they kindly shared their knowledge with me. They warned me that I would need several million euros to launch a new brand. I didn't have that money, and the road that we had chosen was longer than that of traditional brands, which don't deal with long research processes and development of unknown plant production chains.

While money was short, I had the support of the best cosmetologist in France and a motivated team, so we began researching. Sometimes, France can be seen as a complicated country for entrepreneurs. However, it is a country that offers huge support to innovation. The support from national agencies was decisive for our three years of research and development.

Then, at the end of 2009, we launched the company into the market and got a very positive market response. We also received strong support from the press, much needed for us to become known, especially with money constraints. But the crisis hit Europe. We experienced hardships which could have killed us: an order cancelled by a large, famous perfume store chain which was already advertised in the media, hiring a mentally unstable employee who made us pay for her issues . . .

But I learnt there is an opportunity in every crisis. The chain store cancellation helped me understand that perhaps we should consider developing a more direct contact with our customers and offer them a broader experience, including massage—an aspect which we started researching.

Little by little we earned a reputation for developing top-quality formulas and other companies asked us to develop products for them. While at first, we had not planned this activity, we welcomed it since it helps us discover new fields and the associated resources provide for Aïny's harmonious growth instead of pursuing volume growth at any cost.

Today, our company is break-even, but we are analysing our next challenge. Based on our history, our eyes are set on the potential of Latin America, but this time as a market. There is no high-end, top brand telling the history of the continent. It is a big challenge, since

Latin Americans don't always value the knowledge and products of their countries. But that's our goal.

Outlook

We want to develop a strong presence in Latin America both as a market and as a source of responsible scientific innovation.

We want to create new store models which combine magic, traditional knowledge, and science. China manages to get a perfect blend of tradition and modernity, and I think we can also make that happen in this continent.

We will continue researching into new plants and massage therapies with a humble attitude and grateful to those who share this knowledge with us.

In just five years, I witnessed a change in the corporate discourse on biodiversity and respect for traditional knowledge and wisdom. My first lectures didn't have a good response from professionals. Challenging patents and giving voice to native communities were going against long-standing industry practices. Over the past years, things changed. Now, large companies argue that they respect native communities and explain everything they do in favour of biodiversity. A great change . . . but is it honest and true? Maybe, now that the idea is no longer brand new, civil society will be in charge of checking compliance with these commitments. What are our next steps? Our role in the cosmetics industry is to make both scientific and social innovations.

I think it's interesting for native communities to have a bigger participation in the appraisal of their knowledge. We want to promote, if they want to, the emergence of the communities' own brands by offering them technical advice. But this will take time as it is quite a stride to make. Besides, I think native communities should create a seal to certify that plants from their territories used by third parties are 'biopiracy free' plants. For the first time, this certification would not be defined by a third-party, such as fair or organic trade, but by the players themselves. However, I know that indigenous leaders are facing big challenges in the short term, such as the protection of their land.

From a scientific side, I find it interesting that healers look at the shape of a leaf to learn what the plant cures. They find their inspiration in nature to create and innovate. A branch of science does exactly the same: biomimicry. For instance, swimsuits which reduce drag in the water were created inspired by shark skin. In the same way, we can develop highly technical, more effective and more sustainable creams. This will be our challenge for the years ahead.

4

Pachacuti, UK

Carry Somers
Company founder and director

Pachacuti is a pioneer in ethical fashion, practising Fair Trade since 1992, and since then we have kept on pushing the boundaries of what is possible within the fashion supply chain, aiming to provide a role model to challenge compromise and mediocrity within the industry. At Pachacuti, we believe that authentic luxury incorporates both social and environmental responsibility without compromising on style. Pachacuti is unfortunately still something of a rarity: a company which adheres to the highest Fair Trade and environmental standards and yet is sold in some of the most luxurious stores around the world.

I am often asked how I became interested in the Andean region and I only wish that I could remember what sparked my initial interest. I can remember asking for a book on the Incas as a Christmas present in my early teens and receiving an impressively fat book for a teenager fascinated by Peru but, for the next decade or so, the Incas were to remain an abstract concept. I went to a conventional Grammar school where subjects like anthropology were not even mentioned in our occasional careers lessons, so a more conventional route was taken through Languages and Modern European Studies.

Finally, my opportunity arose; I discovered a Master's in Native American Studies being run at the University of Essex. Based in the Department of Art History and Theory and taught by a renowned group of experts in the field, I spent a year delving into every topic of personal interest, from the Misquito Coast of Nicaragua to the post-conquest Peruvian chronicles of Guaman Poma de Ayala. In tutorials with the PhD students, I was amazed and intrigued by the complexities of the Mayan calendar, while learning Quechua taught me about subtleties of language which I had never imagined. One concept which I found particularly interesting is that there is no word for possession in Quechua. Everything which you 'have' in English is, instead, either with you, or not with you. This means that, for the Quechua speaker, you are the steward of things, not the owner. Certainly an important concept to consider where sustainability is concerned.

For my dissertation research, I travelled to Ecuador to look at textile production and the continuation of traditional skills and techniques since pre-Columbian times. When I started talking to the producers, I was shocked to learn the extent to which middlemen controlled the textile industry and the difficulties which small producers faced. Seeing the weighing scales, an international symbol of justice, being loaded with wool on one side and then seeing the producers being charged a price which bore no resemblance to the supposed cost per kilo, I felt a sense of outrage at the clear discrimination being practised before me. Quechua speakers with only rudimentary Spanish and low levels of numeracy were at the mercy of the middlemen when it came both to buying the wool and selling their finished garments. I met two groups of workers who had organised themselves into cooperatives, but both had experienced arson attacks due to the threat which they posed to the intermediaries' monopoly of the supply chain.

I felt very much at home in academia and, if it hadn't been for Pachacuti eventually pulling me away, I would happily have immersed myself in research. The following year was spent sailing on a variety of square riggers in the Caribbean. Dipping into the library in the British Virgin Islands, I managed to put together a proposal for a PhD on 'The Symbolism of Colour in the Andes' and, to my surprise, I subsequently received notification that I had been awarded a full research grant. In April, I arrived back in the UK after two months sailing across the Atlantic in a rather ropy topsail schooner. The next five months stretched ahead of me until my PhD commenced and getting an office job just seemed too confining after spending the previous year climbing the rigging!

If I hadn't picked up Anita Roddick's autobiography and read it in the garden one sunny day after my return, I would undoubtedly have continued in academia and my life would have been very different. But I didn't. I read the book from cover to cover in the garden that day and decided that if one woman could make such a difference in the beauty industry with no experience, there was nothing to stop me from doing the same in the fashion industry, at least in my summer holidays! I was so grateful to have the opportunity to say thank you to Anita Roddick several years later and tell her that, at that time, I was supporting 1,000 women in the Andes as a direct result of reading her book.

Seeing an opportunity to help these producers while earning some holiday money to support my future studies, I decided to return to Ecuador in order to provide training and a sales outlet for the producer groups I had met through my research. I naïvely thought that this could be a worthwhile project and, despite the lack of any design experience, I was fairly sure that I could design knitwear which would be more appealing to the Western market than their current patterns and colour combinations. I had £500 in the bank and borrowed a further £500 from my mother, which was enough for the flight to Ecuador and payment for my first knitwear collection. I took my inspiration from Latin American petroglyphs and cave art, creating a series of knitwear patterns which used natural dyes such as eucalyptus and walnut and beautiful raku ceramic buttons featuring pre-Columbian designs.

1992 saw that rare occurrence in the UK, a very hot summer. My first attempt to sell the boxes of knitwear I had shipped home was at a rather smart family festival in the Devon countryside. In scorching temperatures, I set up a rail outside the faded orange and blue family tent in which I had spent many childhood camping holidays. People walked past me pityingly, not realising that this was my first ever event, commiserating with my misfortune to be selling Ecuadorian wool jumpers during the hottest summer for years. However, unaccustomed to camping, their opinions changed when night fell and the clear skies resulted in freezing temperatures and frequent knocks on the 'door' of the tent to buy a late-night cardigan. After another festival, I had sold out of my stock and ordered a second consignment to be knitted.

I hadn't envisaged the success of my first collection, nor realised the positive impact it would have on my producers' livelihoods, so at the end of the summer I decided to turn down my PhD. I have always been a very decisive person and, after seeing the injustices within the textile industry, I knew that I was one of the few people aware of the situation through my research and believed that I could make a difference in that situation. In the light of this knowledge, continuing with a PhD seemed too selfish a path to follow when the benefit to disadvantaged producers within rural communities in Ecuador seemed considerable.

I named my new business Pachacuti, meaning world upside-down in the Quechua language, as it signified my desire to redress the inequalities in the fashion industry through demonstrating that it was possible to run a successful clothing and accessories business which benefited marginalised producers and was environmentally sustainable. The whole concept of Fair Trade was barely known at this time, far less the term 'ethical fashion'. From the outset, Pachacuti was committed not just to Fair Trade principles, but to the promotion of traditional skills and to community development, focusing on working with women's groups who were economically, socially or geographically marginalised. You could say that it was a very British sense of fair play that started me on my entrepreneurial journey to create the pioneering Fair Trade fashion brand which is Pachacuti today.

Flush from the success of that first summer, I was delighted when a friend's mother agreed to help me with a £5,000 loan to grow the business. However, the first year threw up many unexpected obstacles. An armed robber in Ecuador stole most of my business profits and the aforementioned loan, and two death threats followed warning me not to pursue the thief. Unfortunately the theft coincided with Black Thursday when Britain dropped out of the European Exchange Rate Mechanism and I lost 30% on currency exchange when I took out a further loan to replace the stolen money.

Then the UK went into recession. Never one to give up, I saved money by living in a van for 9 months of the year. This itinerant lifestyle coincided with Margaret Thatcher's Criminal Justice Act, meaning that I was constantly moved on by the police in the middle of the night due to paranoia surrounding traveller convoys as my pea-green van was hard to miss when parked up in a village lay-by. Although I had no intention of joining a convoy and was using my van to drive to fairs around the country to sell my knitwear, the police had new powers to move on anyone driving a 'suspicious' vehicle. It wasn't an easy start, but I'm not easily deterred!

The future direction of Pachacuti was determined by one passing visitor at the Global Christmas Fair in Olympia at which I was exhibiting in 1992. My stand displayed a mixture of knitwear and accessories, but in the corner, rather unseasonally for November, I was selling a couple of Panama hats. A buyer from the Conran Shop walked past and expressed an interest in rollable Panama hats and, shortly after, my first order from the Conran Shop arrived. For many years, the Conran Shop was Pachacuti's main source of revenue and our hats became the best-selling item in their gardening department in London, Paris and Japan. Twenty-one years later, the Conran Shop remains one of Pachacuti's best clients and I would like to think that the longevity of this relationship is a testimony to Pachacuti's high standards of quality and design.

A surprise encounter over lunch in Ecuador in 1993 resulted in a business partner who provided a much-needed injection of cash, as well as some welcome assistance at fairs and events over the summer months. However, as someone who has all of the characteristics of a typical entrepreneur, it was not easy for me to negotiate and compromise; I was far too stubborn and opinionated. However, meeting Alan did lead to a slightly easier way of life as we decided to open Pachacuti's first shop in Exeter; something which would never have happened without his investment in the business. Eventually we amicably parted ways and I spent the next few years repaying the investment and share of profits.

I am often asked when Pachacuti started breaking even, but we always made a profit from the outset. Any profits were reinvested into the business in order to fund future growth. I look with a mixture of envy and pity at ethical businesses who have managed to garner high levels of investment; it must be exciting to have the money to realise different projects and build the business at a faster pace, but at the same time this means that you are accountable to your investors and can incur high levels of interest which can sap profits. My desire has always been to demonstrate that it is possible to be a profitable fashion brand while adhering to the highest standards of quality and ethics throughout the supply chain.

Growing sustainably may not be the route to high turnover and quick profits, but it does ensure that the business is solid and stable, both for ourselves in the UK and for our producer groups. Long-term relationships are an important concept of Fair Trade and I am very proud of the fact that we have been working with some of our producer groups since 1992 and they have expanded in parallel with our growth. Until the economic downturn in the past few years, our turnover was growing at around 15% per annum which seems a really manageable figure for both Pachacuti's staff and for our producer groups who are able to expand gradually to cope with increased demand. In fact, when we looked at the membership figures for our Panama hat association, it grew by 15% per annum as well in line with our increased sales! Working with associations and cooperatives, democratic membership organisations, expanding production means taking on new members, with all of the mutual commitment which that entails, so our producer groups need to be sure that growth will be sustained in order to enrol new members.

In 1996 a new chapter in Pachacuti's metamorphosis began when I moved to Derbyshire, opened a shop in Ashbourne, and my beautiful daughter Sienna was born. Juggling the demands of what was soon to be single-motherhood, together with working an 80 hour week, was never going to be easy and I look back on those times wondering how I ever managed to keep the business going. Literally all of my profits were spent on childcare costs; from 6 weeks old Sienna spent 10 hours every day with a childminder. However, I knew that it was not just my daughter who was dependent on me, but the families of all of our producer groups, many of whom were only at school due to my payment of their matriculation fees each term. I literally had no disposable income at all: I bought one babygro for Sienna from a charity shop and all the rest were hand-me-downs, while haggling with the supermarket manager for discounts as the store closed at night became the norm. The first years of Sienna's life were just a matter of business survival with time and money being equally precious as both were in very short supply. Pachacuti was solid, stable and profitable, just not profitable enough!

At this stage of the business, I hadn't set out a social and environmental strategy for Pachacuti. I could see the positive difference we were making on the ground, not just in Ecuador, but by now in Peru and Bolivia, but our work with producer groups remained quite reactionary. We helped them financially when they came to us asking for assistance, or if we saw issues which needed addressing in order to improve social and environmental standards, but this was done in a fairly unplanned way and the money and time invested in producer development frequently went unrecorded.

My daughter Sienna came with me on my trips to Ecuador from an early age and I always appreciated the sense of community among my producers as I was never short of someone to look after her while I worked on my designs. On the morning of September 11, 2001, I had just arrived in Ecuador with Sienna. Unbeknownst to me at the time, my future husband first saw me that morning as his flight back to the US had been cancelled and he had driven into town to watch news coverage of 9/11, before sitting on a rooftop terrace to drown his sorrows. From this vantage point, he spotted Sienna and me skipping across the square and, the following day, we turned up at the fabric company where he was working. After a transatlantic relationship for the next few years, Mark eventually moved to the UK and has since been working with me at Pachacuti, using his design and IT skills to direct our marketing strategy, from building Pachacuti's website to designing lookbooks to helping with product design and production.

I remember deciding one day, not long after meeting Mark, sitting in the tiny courtyard garden behind my shop, that I would give the business another three years and, if I could not turn it around and make it a real success, I would become a French teacher. Back-up plan in place, I finally began to put together a business plan, something I had never done before, and soon realised the importance of having a vision of where I wanted Pachacuti to go, setting out our social, economic and environmental objectives and working out how to get there. Hats were becoming increasingly important as part of our sales, both for retail and wholesale, and our website www.panamas.co.uk which, as the name suggests was focused on Panama hats, started to generate a significant proportion of our sales.

At this stage, I was still designing and selling seasonal ranges of clothing and knitwear, including Peruvian and Bolivian alpaca, hand-batiked dresses and hand-embroidered blouses. Pachacuti was the world's first Fair Trade hat specialist but I resisted focusing entirely on felt and Panama hats as I knew that we had so many other small producer groups dependent on us and one of the main aims of Pachacuti's work has always been the promotion of cultural heritage through the preservation of traditional skills. However, it was the Panama hats which were increasingly moving to the forefront, both in terms of sales and business profile.

Behind the classic Panama hat lies a history of centuries of exploitation meaning that hat weaving is rapidly dying out; but the higher prices paid by Pachacuti had led to a waiting list for membership at our main weaving association and we started working with a second women's cooperative in order to meet demand. Pachacuti Panama hats are made from organically grown *Carludovica palmata* sourced from a community-owned plantation which encourages biodiversity of plants and animals. Once a plant is established it grows to full height every 30 days and can be cropped once a month for 100 years. Nothing is wasted; fibres not suitable for Panama hats are used for roofing. Until fairly recently the straw was carried out of the plantations by donkey, but the communities now hire trucks to collect the straw. First, the tender leaves are cooked in the coastal communities, often by the family members of the men who cut the straw. The leaves are then dried indoors, after which they curl up vertically and form narrow cylindrical fibres. Once processed, the straw is transported to the weaving communities, either on the coast or in the highlands where our weaving groups are located.

The Panama hat industry has always been dominated by *perros* ('dogs' in Spanish) whose unscrupulous purchasing methods force the weavers to accept a very low price for their labour. The weavers' lack of business knowledge can also exacerbate the problem as they are often prone to ignoring long-standing relationships in favour of ready cash. With a Pachacuti Panama, the women carry out the entire production process within the association, from weaving to finishing, and the absence of middlemen means that the association retains more of the final value of the hat and can therefore provide more benefits to its members, such as healthcare and pensions.

Without the certainty of a regular income resulting from Pachacuti's year-round ordering policy, many of our weavers would be forced to move to urban centres or migrate to the US to look for low-paid domestic work and would begin to lose touch with their cultural heritage. Pachacuti's Fair Trade purchasing provides a sustainable livelihood, enabling them to remain within their rural communities where they can fit hat weaving around the agricultural cycle and caring for their families. This is particularly important in a community where 60% of children have at least one parent living overseas, which has led to the devastation of families, high rates of alcoholism, youth suicide and teenage pregnancies, coupled with declining school performance.

Pachacuti supports an ever-expanding pension scheme for our weavers (their average age is 55) as well as projects such as our annual glasses for glasses programme, run in conjunction with Ashbourne schools, which pays for glasses and cataract operations for all producers who require them. However, Pachacuti believes that Fair Trade should benefit the whole community wherever possible, not just the people who are fortunate enough to work for us. Pachacuti has supported Alcoholics Anonymous in the village, helped our weavers establish a community grocery store and, for several years, our weaving association housed an office administering almost 200 grants to encourage child workers to return to school, grants for disabled young people and a centre providing a lawyer, psychologist and social worker.

As we measure our impact, it has shown that social and economic improvements can play a vital part in improving not just their standard of living, but also levels of self-esteem and sense of well-being for our producers in Ecuador. Furthermore, we are helping to affirm their indigenous identity through the preservation of their traditional skills, skills which are under threat of extinction unless a fair wage is paid to the weavers. As part of our current social strategy, now that we have decided to become more focused solely on hats, we are trying to incorporate as many traditional skills from Fair Trade sources as possible into our hat production, so our felt and Panama hats are using an assortment of hand-woven and hand-batiked ribbons, cow horn buckles, beaded bands, tagua nut trims and silver charms, all produced locally in Ecuador by traditional, rural craftspeople.

Looking back, I believe the real turning point for Pachacuti was our selection by the World Fair Trade Organisation (WFTO) as a pilot for the Sustainable Fair Trade Management System (SFTMS). I had always thought that, if a certification system was introduced for handicraft products, as opposed to the Fairtrade certification for commodities, the Panama hat would be the ideal first product to bear the mark as it once epitomised colonial rule, while a Fair Trade Panama hat would symbolise that power had been returned to the hands of the producers.

Pachacuti does not use any commodities covered by the Fairtrade mark, so certification seemed an important means of differentiating ourselves in an increasingly crowded ethical marketplace. I also believed that a certification covering the entire supply chain represented vitally important progress within the fashion industry where added value is not determined predominantly by raw materials but by all the processes involved in the creation of the finished article. Indeed, many of the well-publicised abuses within the fashion industry in recent years have occurred in the factories which are sewing the garments or in the embellishment stage when nimble-fingered children are employed to sew on sequins.

The SFTMS brought a systematic approach to our social and environmental work with our producers. It provided both a framework and a focus so that Fair Trade principles became the core of our decision-making processes. In order to receive our certification, we had to demonstrate sustainable management practices and continuous improvement in each of the ten Fair Trade principles. In fact, 11 in the case of Pachacuti as we have always included the Preservation of Cultural Heritage as an additional key principle relevant to our work with Andean producers. Implementing and adopting a demanding international standard such as the SFTMS within a small business is a huge challenge. It has been worthwhile in the long term as it is a very comprehensive management system which ensures social and environmental sustainability, but it was very time consuming as we had to develop the analytical tools and methodology in order to obtain feedback in simple, visual form as only 37% of our producers have completed primary education.

Tools were developed to analyse the entire production process, including raw materials mapping, eco-mapping (production, waste, chemicals, energy, water) and production flow charts with the aim of reducing non-compliances, identifying health & safety issues and ascertaining where quality checks needed to be strengthened. These tools improved our understanding of the entire supply chain and, together with our producers, we analysed where improvements need to be made and create an annual action plan. These annual plans with each producer group, as well as for Pachacuti in the UK, worked towards an overarching three-year plan.

As an ethical fashion pioneer, I believe that it is important that we do not become complacent but continue to push standards higher within the fashion industry. After becoming the world's first certified Fair Trade organisation, Pachacuti piloted the EU Geo Fair Trade project from 2009 to 2012, which was aimed at providing visible accountability of sustainable provenance. Transparency and traceability urgently needs to be improved within supply chains in order to avoid anonymity and, as a consequence, human rights, labour and environmental infringements, and no more so than within the fashion industry. Pachacuti staff were involved in collecting around 100 social, economic and environmental indicators, tracking progress over several years. The collection of geolocalisation data enabled us to trace production to the GPS coordinates of each weaver's house, not easy data to collect when only 45% of our weavers' houses are accessible by road. This level of traceability is intended to enhance the trust of consumers in their intention to support the sustainable development of communities while enabling them to see the impact of their purchases on the livelihoods of producer groups. Our weavers are delighted that this helps correct a historical misnomer as consumers can track Panama hats back to their country of origin, Ecuador!

The most recent stage in our certification journey has been our participation in the pilot for the new WFTO Fair Trade Guarantee System which entailed audits both in the UK and in Ecuador against the WFTO Fair Trade Standard. As with the SFTMS, we are continuing to create economic, social and environmental improvement plans both for Pachacuti and for our producer groups for the new system. In the UK, our objectives include the purchase of specialist hat sewing machines, expanding our hat customisation options and building a garden of raised beds in our courtyard so that staff can grow salad crops for lunch. In Ecuador, we plan to build capacity by increasing the active membership of our current women's association, encouraging more young women to join so that Panama hat weaving does not die out. We also aim to put in place a long-term strategy to improve continuity as this can be difficult to achieve in democratic organisations where the management may change annually. Launched at London Fashion Week in September 2013, Pachacuti and People Tree became the first fashion companies in the world to be awarded the new WFTO Fair Trade label.

We believe that it is important to back up our Fair Trade claims with indicators showing the real impact we are having on our producers, which is why participation in these schemes has been an integral part of our management process over the past few years. However, we do not just look down the supply chain, but we also examine all of our operations in the UK with the aim of ensuring that all products and services are sourced as ethically and sustainably as possible. In order to be an accountable business, we annually measure all of our CO_2 emissions from travel, freight (import, export, courier, post) and energy use in our Ashbourne headquarters. We have reduced Pachacuti's overall CO_2 emissions by 27.5% in the past 2 years and energy usage in our shop premises has reduced by 49% in past 5 years. As well as switching our shop lighting to a system which could use eco halogens, we have also switched to a 100% renewables tariff for our electricity and received the UK's first green gas from Ecotricity.

It has always been important for us at Pachacuti to integrate our commercial objectives with our social and environmental strategy. For instance, the more fashion forward collections of Panama hats which we have developed over the past five years, with a diversity of weaves, patterns and bright colours, has come directly from our action plan with our women's weaving association. The action plan to develop this side of our collection came, in turn, from worker feedback during our annual assessment which revealed that many of the older weavers were unable to weave the finer hats due to arthritis and poor eyesight. Moreover, we also conducted a time trial to calculate how long it took to weave a hat as, through interview methodology, weavers claimed that a grade 2 Panama hat took over 18 hours but, by conducting a 2-day time trial following natural weaving rhythms, we arrived at just over 8 hours average per hat! Not only did this data allow us to more accurately evaluate prices paid, but we also discovered through the time trial that the women could weave a coloured or patterned hat one hour faster than a natural hat. So really, our participation in Fashion Weeks around Europe with our hat collections can be seen as the direct result of the needs of our weavers as, without their feedback, we may still be focusing on the fine, rollable, ivory-coloured Panama hats which fewer and fewer of them are able to weave.

Participating in London, Paris and Milan Fashion Week has been integral to Pachacuti's growth as a luxury brand as it is this exposure which has helped to launch us into the Japanese market and we are now sold in the foremost luxury stores in Tokyo. Japan is now our main export market, with exports growing to other Far East countries such as Singapore, Thailand, Taiwan, Korea and China. Luxury retailers and consumers are our customers and we need to understand the nuances of this market to better serve them. As a result, in 2012 and 2013 Pachacuti participated in a UK Fashion and Textiles fashion trade mission to Japan which provided us with an opportunity to visit current customers, such as Isetan and Matsuya, which are among the foremost luxury stores in Japan.

Our previous three-year plan was to increase exports to ten additional countries by 2012 and we achieved 21. In addition to the growing Far East market, we now have stockists in Australia, Austria, Belgium, Canada, Denmark, France, Germany, Greece, Italy, Lebanon, Mexico, Netherlands, New Zealand, Poland, Romania, Russia, Spain, Sweden, Switzerland, the Caribbean and the USA. In addition to retail shops, we also supply many notable organisations and venues such as Highgrove, English Heritage, Goodwood and Glyndebourne Opera.

Another of our commercial strategies which is being driven by social objectives is the growth in our private label work. The main reason we have worked to increase our private label collaborations with major brands is because it is an excellent way of providing large orders to our weavers earlier in the season and helps to ensure year-round consistency of purchasing levels. Over the past five years, Pachacuti has brought Fair Trade to Savile Row, creating the Gieves & Hawkes classic Panama hat collection, created an eye-popping range of private label hats for Paul Smith, as well as designs for Brora, Hiroko Koshino, Cath Kidston, Monsoon, Johnstons of Elgin and our first bag collection for Livia Firth Designs for YOOX.

Pachacuti saw the recession as an opportunity to redefine our brand and carve out a niche for ourselves. We carried out a brand refresh with a new logo and fresh look, accompanied by a new website for both retail and trade customers and, most importantly, consolidated our product range around hats and travel accessories. We feel well-placed for the future to gain customers from the traditional market, bespoke tailors for example, as well as targeting new hat wearers through the expansion of our fashion collections. We decided to move Pachacuti's products up the brand 'ladder' to appeal to a more premium and luxury consumer. This process has been very successful and has allowed us to raise wages and increase benefit to our producers in accordance with our Fair Trade principles.

As a brand, we have found it increasingly challenging to know how we should combine the Fair Trade story alongside our Britishness and the refined, aspirational messaging associated with luxury marketing. Our customers do not buy from us just because we are an ethical brand, but instead they choose our products for their design, beautiful materials and fine craftsmanship. Pachacuti has always championed artisanal skills: our hand-blocked felt hats and Panamas use bespoke trims such Luton grosgrain, Devon silk jacquard, Dashing Tweeds and feathers sourced from Scottish game estates. It is part of our brand's mission to source ethically and locally throughout the entire supply chain to the benefit of local communities and the preservation of local industries, as well as supporting our Fair Trade producers in Ecuador. All of our materials are consciously sourced for their environmental and social impact, thus contributing to a more sustainable design aesthetic.

In the past we have tended to rely on our ethical story for our marketing as this has always been at the core of our business. However, as we have expanded our exports, we are increasingly marketing ourselves as a British brand. British design is well known for both its innovation and heritage and Pachacuti expresses this well as a brand. We feel that creating and marketing British-designed luxury products with bespoke British trims will be the key to Pachacuti's further growth and success.

My work focus has shifted considerably since April 2013 and our fantastic team have taken on most of the day-to-day running of Pachacuti. In the days following the catastrophic collapse of the Rana Plaza garment factory in Bangladesh and the ever-growing death toll, many articles appeared urging consumers to support ethical fashion as a way to improve working conditions throughout the supply chain. The momentum was considerable, but how best to build on this energy and sudden spike in interest and turn it into a longstanding campaign which could bring about real change within the industry? A few days later, I had the idea to create an annual Fashion Revolution Day on the anniversary of the disaster and this has since grown into a global movement, taking place around the world, mobilising the entire value chain, from cotton farmers and garment workers, through to brands and consumers. Led by brands, retailers, campaigners, press and academics from within the sector and beyond, we will celebrate good practice, raise awareness of the true cost of fashion and continue to campaign for change. In December 2013 I was honoured to receive the Outstanding Contribution to Sustainable Fashion Award at the House of Lords in recognition of my work both at Pachacuti and Fashion Revolution Day.

As a pioneer in ethical fashion, Pachacuti's aim is to provide our customers with truly sustainable luxury, creating designs which look good and endure not just from season to season, but from decade to decade. We are working to ensure continuity of quality standards across all of our Fair Trade producer groups, so that we can meet the continued challenges of producing sustainable products with marginalised rural producer groups which are destined for the world's top luxury markets. We will endeavour not only to provide our customers with fashion accessories to meet their aspirations, but also to become a brand which brings them inspiration as we believe that authentic luxury should bring positive benefit to all affected by its creation.

5

We Are Knitters, Spain

María José Marín
Company co-founder and director

When I received my degree, I started working at PwC as a financial auditor. I was only 21 years old and already had the 'We Are Knitters' idea in mind. That is why I knew PwC would be a temporary job from the very beginning. Reading that, it is logical to think that I was not motivated enough during my period as auditor. On the contrary, I put all my efforts in to learn everything I could. Auditing was with no doubt a very profitable experience and very suitable for any entrepreneur. Actually, when I decided to apply to PwC, people did not understand my choice since I had never really liked accounting or finance during my degree, but I had read it was a good education for entrepreneurs and it definitely was.

All that accounting and the know-how I acquired elaborating balances and P&Ls was a huge help when financing We Are Knitters.

Since I was a little kid, I wanted to do something creative, to build something. After finishing school, I had no idea what path to follow. I had no vocation so I studied international business, spending the first two years in France between Reims and Paris. In my second year, one professor told us the story of two alumni that succeeded in starting a business. For the first time I thought, I want to build my own business.

More than a business, I wanted to create a brand. Once I finished college and before I started to work at PwC, I spent my summer browsing on the Internet trying to find something that inspired me. I remember I was already obsessed with wool. I have always loved the noble fibres. I found a lot of amazing websites and businesses that revolved around wool; some of them were amazing. I found that other people were operating differently from fast fashion companies such as Zara or H&M: using noble and natural fibres such as wool, cashmere, even vicuña wool. I looked for inspiration proactively.

A lot of them inspired me in the process but maybe one impressed me the most: Loro Piana.

This Italian fashion brand produces luxury garments made with the most precious raw materials in the world: the vicuña from Peru or cashmere from Mongolia among others. They focus on finding the best quality fleeces around the world and promoting the sustainable production of the wool, preserving endangered species such as vicuña. The long history and the values and practices of Loro Piana were with no doubt inspiration for We Are Knitters.

I was completely seduced by the production process of the wool and the wool itself. All our investigations led us to one place: Peru. Peru has wool yarns that are second to none. The production process is almost an art. We loved the quality, tradition and the craftsmanship around the wool in Peru. We knew our raw materials would come from this amazing country.

The colours of Peru, its people, its landscapes, everything became inspiring for us. In some localities of the Peruvian Andes, knitting is a way of living: all the women know how to knit and men raise alpacas, llamas and sheep.

We knew very early that We Are Knitters would be very attached to this wonderful country and we look forward to being more involved with the local communities and cooperatives in the near future.

There is a long way to go to improve local working conditions and quality of life by setting up a sustainable production system.

The investigation started without any particular idea in mind. And then, in a trip to New York, I discovered that knitting there was a huge trend among young and cool people. It was there, in New York, where the idea was really outlined: more than designing and producing clothes, there was a clear opportunity in the DIY market in Europe. The aim of doing business with Peruvian wool and the DIY trend led to the actual concept of We Are Knitters: a knitting brand. But not a usual knitting brand; we really wanted to differentiate our commitment and ourselves not only with the raw materials produced by local communities in Peru but also with the image of the brand. Our strategy was to produce fashionable and high-end collections and catalogues. We wanted to become a luxury knitting brand.

Deciding to start the business

One day, in early 2011, I woke up after having slept little due to PwC work and I knew that the idea of We Are Knitters was already developed and waiting to be transformed into a real project. To keep my well-paid job as an auditor was incompatible with the success of We Are Knitters. I was very clear that I could never put 100% into both and I hate to do things by halves. I put too much passion and effort in what I do. It was time to make one of the most important decisions I have made in my life.

I was still very young with nothing (other than a monthly salary) to lose and a lot to win. I realised that I knew how my life was going to be if I continued at PwC—my track and evolution—and it definitely did not attract me. On the other hand to start a project like We Are

Knitters was full of uncertainties, yet exciting. I was thrilled having just won an entrepreneurship price from my university ICADE with an award of €10,000 to invest.

In the process of outlining the idea, the person who helped me the most was Alberto Bravo, the other half of We Are Knitters. We met at PwC; I told him I had seen a huge knitting trend in New York among young and trendy people and that I always wanted to run my own business. I quickly proposed him to be my partner. Alberto was one of my best friends and he still is. We started to investigate the trend and in a few weeks we knew everything about knitting, wool and needles. The more we knew the more interested we were.

We were very young with almost no experience but we had a lot of motivation, intuition and energy. We teamed up to build We Are Knitters. This is one of the keys to the success of a project, to team with the right partner. Alberto and I are very complementary in our skills and roles in We Are Knitters. If I had to give only one piece of advice to entrepreneurs it would be to choose the right partner; even if it sounds like a cliché, it is really one of the keys to success. It is extremely important to be aligned in the vision and strategy of the enterprise and to have complementary skills.

Alberto and I did not have relevant experience before building the brand but we started with a passion, perseverance and energy, which were enough to launch the brand in Spain and succeed in it. The unknown cannot be a barrier; everything can be learned, more so nowadays as we have such easy access to information.

Before launching We Are Knitters, we were both working at PwC as auditors. Even though our actual work now has nothing in common with our former employment, it is true that the experience acquired in PwC gave us a superb working methodology and rigour that helped us now and in the beginning to resolve all kinds of obstacles.

For Alberto and me, We Are Knitters meets our personal and professional ambitions, which is very important in the execution and success of the business. We work in the company that we dreamt of, a company that links together craftsmanship, tradition and sustainability with creativity, luxury and fashion. We are very proud of it even though we have to improve some aspects of it.

We were positively surprised at how the market loved the purity of natural wool and ventured into a new activity that had been outdated for so many years. We could not be more satisfied by the response of the knitters: both the beginners who wanted to try a new activity and the advanced knitters who appreciated the exceptional nature of the yarns and patterns.

The inception of We Are Knitters

In the inception and early days of We Are Knitters, I was living in New York, immersed in a city full of creativity, having just left my previous job and with the first challenge facing us. We had to build from scratch a product, a website, a name and, ultimately, a brand. Nevertheless, I knew I was in the right place, the centre and origin of the knitting movement and trend.

I do not know when exactly We Are Knitters stopped being a project or an idea and became a reality. I remember that six months passed and we had the first version of what we are now. We spent six months finding the right suppliers, designing the products, building the website . . .

We spent a lot of time on the Internet; it was our best way to understand the logistics process and to learn. We just observed how other comparable, online, e-commerce companies were doing it and watched videos of other fashion companies' founders. Nowadays, it is very easy to get information via the Internet. We could get very valuable information and knowledge online, but we had to be careful and picked the right information and advice from other entrepreneurs. We found the first providers on the Internet. Some other entrepreneurs also helped us; their advice and experience were extremely valuable for us and helped us to avoid typical mistakes. The most important one was not waiting until the product was perfect to launch it.

Indeed, when we launched in 2011, we had more of a beta-version than a real product. This allowed us to build it with a very low budget and use market feedback to finish our product. This is the best way to know if something is going to work: launching it even if it is not perfect and using the response and feedback of the consumers to improve it and finish it.

With very little capital, we built the first version of We Are Knitters and word of mouth was enough to start the knitting movement in Spain. We very quickly acquired hundreds of loyal and returning users. When trying and succeeding to make this project happen, one of the keys was that we were very focused on the execution. When starting a project, nothing happens unless you make it happen. And we did it quickly but wisely, controlling all the phases and studying all the steps before taking them.

Maybe the biggest challenges were the logistics and operations (importing, stocking, shipping to the customers, etc.) and the marketing and getting known (with a very low budget).

First steps

At the beginning, Alberto, my co-founder, and I had to make a lot of important decisions that now define the brand and us.

The most important was about the wool yarn and the sourcing of it. We asked some friends what they thought about the idea: selling knit-it-yourself kits for both beginners and experienced knitters with amazing and colourful wool. Everyone seemed to be very enthusiastic until the price of the kit came into the conversation. Some of them found it a little pricey or did not understand that the purpose of DIY is not just to save money.

We did not just want to sell a product but mainly an experience. The luxurious experience of having a good time doing something by yourself, to disconnect, to spend time on you or thinking about the person you are going to give the hand-knitted clothes to.

We wanted a good yarn so you can keep the garment you knitted by yourself all your life. Our intention was to source our raw materials in Peru with the softest yarn; we really wanted to make the knitting experience unforgettable.

One reason that explains our early success is that we were from the beginning very focused on the execution. We made it happen. Our family and friends, who didn't believe at that time 100% in our idea, helped us.

In Spain, entrepreneurship it is not culturally accepted as a success or even as 'real work', so we had to deal with a lot of unbelievers, people around us who did not understand how we could leave a very good job as auditors to do something full of uncertainty. But Alberto and I were 200% sure and convinced of what we were doing and we convinced our relatives that what we were doing was not mad.

It is, by far, the most important choice we have made, professionally, to date. I am very satisfied with the change and my new professional challenge. Even though it is very demanding and we have both made a lot of personal concessions, it is with no doubt a very satisfying and fulfilling experience that has changed our lives forever.

We definitely weren't satisfied with the first version of the website or the product, but as entrepreneurs we are never satisfied with it even now; we always tend to make a lot of changes. Nevertheless, I received some very valuable advice that I want to share here: try it and then you will see the response of the market, don't wait to have the perfect product. Otherwise you will spend money and time without knowing if people like it and are willing to try it.

In the very beginning, we weren't satisfied; we had to improve in our environmental strategy. From the conception of We Are Knitters, we clearly had consciousness of the environment and as we put it into practice, we realised how difficult it can be to do so and to maintain your convictions.

The first difficulty that we encountered was that it was very difficult to find the quality of yarn that we wanted. Peru is far from Spain and we did not count on a travel budget. Online it was not possible to test the yarn, the quality of it and how it is produced. We finally found a wonderful supplier that met all our requirements and provides us with one of the best wools in the world, of which we are very proud. We recently changed our wool supplier to one that is more in accordance with our values in producing the wool.

The wool was the pillar of the project and embodies the social and environmental commitment of We Are Knitters. It was very important to find exceptional and natural wool preserving the ancient activity of the locals in Peru.

Besides the yarn, we wanted to produce wooden knitting needles instead of plastic or metal. This was necessary as it was the most environmental friendly material for our thick knitting needles. We found a supplier in Spain who just met our requirements for craftsmanship and environmental responsibility. Our supplier is accredited by the PEFC (Programme for the Endorsement of Forest Certification) to ensure our commitment to sustainability.

The packaging is also a very important element of the knitting kit. Our 'knitters' absolutely love it and they re-use it for other purposes than containing wool yarn. This was our goal: to pack the kit in something environmentally friendly. The best material was the paper bag, a simple and cool packaging emulating the traditional market paper bag and very easy to re-use.

Now, we would like to be more in touch with and offer more help to the local communities. We would love to interact directly with the cooperatives and communities in the Peruvian Andes, where knitting is a way of living. In that sense, we haven't entirely satisfied our social project.

We Are Knitters today

We Are Knitters is a luxury knitting online shop and knitters community. We do not only sell knitting products but also experiences. Luxury experiences. To create something that you can use with your own hands has become, nowadays, a true privilege. We provide moments of entertainment and happiness; this is why our slogan is 'all the happiness in a kit'.

I read the book by the founder of TOMS Shoes and he said that, instead of customers, he had supporters. We also do; our clients are more than just customers, they not only buy our kits or knitting materials but they come back to the web or to the social networks to share the result of their knitting project with us or even to show us the progress of the knitting and how much they are enjoying it.

We provide knitters with knitting kits with 100% Peruvian wool in winter and 100% Pima cotton in summer. The kits are divided into four levels from the beginner to the advanced knitter (beginner, easy, intermediate and advanced); all can find their kit and style.

The knitting kits contain all you need to knit the chosen model: the yarn balls, the wooden needles, the pattern, a small knitter's sewing needle and a We Are Knitters tag. We also distribute yarn balls of wool and cotton and wooden needles separately.

We choose the colours very carefully each season. We always pick some basic colours like natural or grey but we also choose colours inspired by Peru: orange, turquoise, yellow . . .

The colours of the yarn along with its exceptional quality make the main advantage and differentiation of the brand. The wool and cotton with its colour, texture and softness make knitting a truly sensitive experience with a modern and fashionable result.

The other differentiation of our business model in comparison with traditional yarn brands is our catalogues. We produce fashionable and magazine-like editorials as catalogues for the brand. This particularity gives the brand a unique and forward-looking image never seen before in a yarn brand. We are bringing a luxurious and modern look to a traditional and antique activity: knitting. This is probably one of the factors that made us succeed in a short period of time. Each new season is a new challenge for us. We have to evolve and add new knitting skills for all levels and, at the same time, get inspiration from the trends in fashion. We get inspiration on the street style as we travel a lot between Madrid, Berlin and London so we have a good idea of the trends.

With our kits and with the brand we make the ultimate trends of the most cosmopolitan cities meet the craftsmanship of some of the most remote villages. This idea inspired us in the inception of the brand and still does when designing the collections and choosing new fibres and materials.

The last characteristic of We Are Knitters is the community aspect of the business among the knitters. On the website, knitters can find video-tutorials for all the levels, complementing the information on our knitting patterns.

Our knitting patterns are made very carefully so even the most inexperienced beginners can understand them.

In 2011, we started selling the kits online. We quickly understood that we needed to sell the yarn balls separately as well, both wool and more recently cotton. Today 50% of the sales are yarns balls. People like to make their own designs or repeat the pattern of the kit in other colours for themselves or to give to someone special.

We also realised that selling our kits in multi-brand fashion stores could be a good strategy to get to people offline, and it worked very well, especially in the holiday season. The kits are a perfect Christmas gift: you can give the kit or the garment knitted by yourself. The best stores in Spain immediately loved our product and made some significant orders. That gave us some brand awareness and recognition.

One thing that determined what we are now is the interaction with the knitters. Actually, the community aspect of We Are Knitters was led by the knitters themselves! They started sharing pictures with us through Facebook or email; now we have an Instagram profile and we have a section on the web called The Knitters, where we post the best Instagram knitting pictures of our clients posted with the hashtag of the brand #weareknitters.

Knitters love to share their knitted projects as they very proud of what they make with their own hands, especially the new beginners who often, before starting, are a little sceptical about their knitting skills.

We have tried since the beginning to improve both our products and our social strategy. When we were building the project, we attended an entrepreneurship event and at a conference we were told to be careful to find a balance between innovation and development. When you are working on the same website or brand we see the same things every day and we tend to change it too often. But we understood that customers do not visit our website so often and it is not worth launching something new every day or week. But still, we always try to be better and more environmentally minded.

The next improvement that we are working on concerns the bag, so that it is not only re-usable and recyclable but also made with recycled paper. This applies to the patterns, too.

From a financial point of view, we were bootstrapped until May 2013. At this moment the structure was very lean and the two of us handled the business ourselves. By then, we had already reached break-even, selling our products mostly in Spain. We could have continued like this and have a profitable business in a few months. But, we were more ambitious and wanted to grow in new countries and conduct new projects with new business lines. This is the reason why we set up a bigger structure and we are still not profitable but instead we are growing internationally and with new product lines.

What's next for us?

We have always wanted to produce already knitted clothes. It will be a new business line, selling hand-knitted clothes. This new line would permit us to be more in contact with Peru, the origin of the yarn. In Peru, the local women are truly knitting experts and they have being doing it since they were children. We Are Knitters would hire those women to knit our exclusive collection. The idea is to help the local communities to produce unique and luxurious garments with their local wool and cotton.

Our plan is to travel to Peru and work together with the local cooperatives, helping and promoting Andean craftsmanship.

This could satisfy the social motivation that we have with this project and help the business with a new line that opens us to a bigger market: the luxury fashion one.

We also have in mind to explore new fibres and yarns. We started recently working with Pima cotton for the summer. Now, we are investigating the introduction of new collections in llama or alpaca yarn in the near future.

6

Positive Luxury, UK

Diana Verde Nieto
Company founder and director

Think of something you've always wanted— to win, to own, to launch, to be . . . Something you've wanted for years. Now imagine you've achieved it—that wonder you've dreamed of every night is yours. How does it feel?

For me, it felt like I'd failed.

Let me put that in context. Back in 2002, when sustainability was even more confusing and unpopular than it is today, I founded a sustainability communications consultancy. We grew from a London-based consultancy to an international agency with offices in Shanghai, New York, Milan and Madrid. We built the company when sustainability was not on people's radars.

I sold the business to a media agency in 2008 and stepped down as CEO in 2010. The buzz of having built and sold a business was short-lived, I had achieved conventional success but I felt like I had failed. For me success is beyond power and money, so I felt that I had not achieved what I had set out to do which was to normalise sustainability.

I had failed to change prevailing attitudes and behaviour towards sustainability, and create a global movement with sustainability at its core. Sustainability had become a dirty word, considered un-chic and inspiring the consumer with nothing but apathy. I wanted to start a business that moved away from the rhetoric of sustainability and instead, became a crusade of positivity (I was taking no prisoners). I wanted to unlock the potential brand value of sustainability and create a platform that allowed consumers to make informed decisions about the brands they were buying from.

Thankfully broader social concern for sustainability has grown from a dull topic in the early 2000s, to a dominant theme today. Leaders of major corporations worldwide are increasingly facing the challenge of managing organisations that meet the expectations of a broad range of stakeholders (often themselves in conflict), while still delivering a substantial return to shareholders. As a result, sustainability is now an essential ingredient for a company's long-term success.

A very high percentage of CEOs see sustainability as a key tool for their company's future success. And to venture one step further, over 50% of them believe that sustainability issues should be fully integrated into the strategy and operations of any company. A sustainable vision is only complete when strong environmental, community and management leadership is part of the foundation. When communities include these leadership elements in the sustainability process, the planning and implementation efforts yield strong economic, social and environmental advancements for today and tomorrow. It is only at this stage that one begins to understand that sustainability is all about bettering people's livelihoods along with their environment. It's a philanthropic love for humanity that identifies values and helps to nourish and develop what is best for all parts involved. Sustainability has to be embedded into a brand's narrative because it is not so much what you do but who you are and how your work contributes to generating a positive difference to the environment and the communities you work in.

After selling my first business I thought I'd never again find something that gets me out of bed without coffee, something that I wanted to give 100% of myself to every day. (My plan B would have been to become an athlete—specifically a long distance runner—but at my age . . . well it is more a dream than any kind of real plan B).

After years of working in the sustainability field, I felt that I should have another go at making sustainability cool, normal and somehow sexy and appealing to a broader spectrum of society. I had the feeling that the sustainability movement could be a lot more successful if we added a touch of positivity, transparency and style.

Positive Luxury was born with the goal of making sustainability cool, sexy and desirable. When working out the bones of the business I was asked to present Sir David Attenborough with his Lifetime Achievement award—and had the pleasure of sitting with him over dinner where, among other things, he told me the story of the blue butterfly—I did not know that the large blue had become extinct from the British Isles in the 1970s. However, it was reintroduced in the 1980s in what is now considered to be one of the greatest feats of reintroduction ever embarked upon. The butterfly was imported from stocks in Sweden and in 2006 an estimated 10,000 were flying in 11 sites.[10]

That's the logo I chose for my new business: an emblem of the positive impact humans can have, that counters all of their negative activities. The blue butterfly demands quality, governance and innovation standards as well as detailed social, environmental and philanthropic efforts. Luxury is no longer about the monetary value of goods or services. Luxury is being redefined as quality products or services that generate the most benefit to all involved in its production and trade.

10 'Large Blue', UK Butterflies, www.ukbutterflies.co.uk/species. php?species=arion, accessed 13 December 2013.

Since the 1970s, complexity and uncertainty surrounding the global environment have increased manifold in light of resource scarcity, significant environmental degradation, and the growing impact and frequency of climate extremes. Consequently, this is influencing purchasing decisions, investment and management decisions.

Needless to say that consumption needs to be understood from a holistic point of view, which encompasses an entire lifestyle influenced by its social context. Behaviour change in consumption is nowadays becoming a conductor for sustainable development policy. However, getting unsustainable consumers to develop more sustainable practices is challenging. Individual behaviour traits are deeply rooted in social and institutional contexts. We are influenced by societal values and a society locked into a cycle of unsustainable habits makes for slow progress. That said, in the grand scheme of things the modern world is unrecognisable from what it was 20 years ago, such has been the abundance of change. When I was a teenager, neither Internet nor smart technology existed and nowadays they are omnipresent in our lives. To an extent the revolution in media and technology has been the catalyst for sustainability to move from the periphery to the core of business strategies. Just as the Internet and what we used to call 'new media' is now the dominant form of mass communications, so has sustainability followed a similar trajectory, from a marginal ideology to a dominant fixture on the business agenda. The two phenomena are co-dependent as the rise in technology has led to a gradual depletion of the world's resources, exerting mounting pressure on finding ways of making sustainability a reality. As this shift in paradigm takes place, I realised that the time was ripe for finding ways to communicate the value of sustainable business to forward-thinking consumers.

What sets Positive Luxury apart from competitors is the fact that it is made up of a very special mix of stakeholders—by means of investors, my team, customers and brands—but what is different is that we recognise that they are all just people and we treat them as such.

My team is very diverse but incredibly complementary. As a true Argentinean I love football and I think the principles of managing a football team are perfect when it comes to the office: everyone with a different strength and skill set, but united by a common goal—the hunger to score and win. I'm a big fan of diversity, not just gender but also cultural. People are diverse and consumers are diverse. If you've nothing in common with your consumers, you're going to struggle to connect with them but if you can replicate their world inside your office you can build a business faster.

This begs a question: Is sustainable leadership different from leadership elsewhere? Leadership, no matter whether it's sustainable or not, is not something you do *to* people but *with* people; hence it works as an exchange and interaction, a two way road, which needs a leader and its followers and all reciprocal actions need to be cultivated, grown and lastly monitored. Anyone, no matter what title or position in society can be a potential leader. Subsequently, we acknowledge the fact that it is something contextual considering that you need to size up and tap into what exists around you and then bring more to the party.

Partners and customers also play a key role. In terms of partners, we've attracted brands that not only talk about being good, but actually *are* good—and not just niche companies, but the likes of H&M, IWC Watches and John Lewis. My ambition is to build a globally recognisable trust mark where all the brands that are investing in bettering people and the planet are displaying the Blue Butterfly Mark of Positive Living next to their products. If there has ever been a high point in the history of Positive Luxury, for me it would be when Rococo Chocolate put the Blue Butterfly Mark of Positive Living on the most sustainable bar of chocolate in the world. What is not to like? I love chocolate—I love Rococo—and, even better, it is sustainable.

I still remember with great pride the moment when the brand Elvis & Kresse was awarded the first Mark of Positive Living. They upcycle luggage, bags, belts and wallets from recycled fire hoses and donate half their profits back to Fire Brigade charities. Mr and Mrs Smith came second. Today, Positive Luxury gets up to 15 requests on a weekly basis from brands that know our project, and would like to be one of our Blue Butterfly Brands. In order for this to be a reality and for us to award the Trust Mark, companies need to undergo a thorough online test that will give us the parameters with which to determine not just their degree of commitment but action against social and environmental practices, good governance, innovation and philanthropic actions.

As you can imagine, a start-up business is very much like a baby—it needs 24/7 attention and dedication in order to grow and develop itself in the right way. Having said that, I am not alone, I have a fantastic team and the support of the brands that are already in the community.

In the beginning, word of mouth was the number one source of new visitors—social media and PR are also helping to spread the word and build the community; nowadays it is a combination of all of the above. It is also the consumers—our consumers spread news and information about brands that share our story as well as their favourite brand narratives. If consumers feel good about the products they buy, they immediately want to share it with the rest of the world, particularly young people. It is here that social media plays a vital and relevant role because it is through these channels that information is accessible and easily re-shared. From the moment something goes viral online, the corporation relinquishes control of the content and this is picked up and appropriated by the consumer. In this way consumers intuitively feel shared content to be a 'pure' and 'trusted' source that makes information easier to understand. It is this particular platform that will enable us to continue to build an active community of brands and consumers, eventually moving towards overseas expansion. Our next stop is the USA in early 2014 and then Asia and Latin America.

We have a clear vision of what we are doing and certainly I think I have learnt a lesson or two by having set up my previous business in five other markets. I learned that flexibility, patience and localisation are the key ingredients to be able to be successful in adapting one's business in other markets—with my team by my side. I am certain that the moment we venture overseas, we will be in a strong position as we have learned a lot already by setting up the business in the UK.

Alongside a good vision and a good team, having the right partners on board makes the whole process much easier. One of the main reasons, I believe, for the current progression for businesses to become so interested in sustainability is that good business practices are sought out by investors. Some investors look for a worthy project, so improving sustainability measures can bring them in.

When I ventured into this project, I was extremely fortunate to have fabulous mentors (I never believed in role models because I don't like putting people on pedestals). Mentoring is sharing successes and failures so you can grow by learning from somebody else's experiences. John Elkington, Jonathon Porritt and Karen Hanton have lived incredibly rich lives and I have been lucky that they have all shared their experiences with me. Consistently, the advice I was given was that you should love yourself, love your project and find a good advisory board as well as constantly take on challenges. Keeping nimble and flexible enough to change while keeping true to the original goal was the major challenge I faced but all this will help entrepreneurs to grow. The most valuable piece of advice that I had was to seek criticism and not to get demotivated by small failures—they are essential to achieving your goal. As a long distance runner I understand what it is to push through pain, but the reward of getting to the finishing line is just too good not to do it.

Recently, I had the opportunity to be a discussion leader at a World Economic Forum workshop organised in London, regarding global growth, innovation and entrepreneurship. The predominant topic of discussion was the issue of entry barriers that students and young adults encounter when trying to set up a business. Being an entrepreneur myself, it was easy to empathise with the points being raised for discussion. I see huge potential for the bettering of support networks for future entrepreneurs in terms of opportunities and available resources. Schools and universities do not teach you how to be an entrepreneur, how to think outside the box and, sometimes, I dare say, how to be comfortable with failure. Although only 50% of start-up businesses will surpass the four year mark, the value of trying and failing is not to be underestimated.

My impression is that people are encouraged to tread the path of caution and are easily sucked into working for big multinationals rather than following the road less travelled. When talking to business leaders, industry experts and colleagues we all agree that the two main challenges entrepreneurs face are funding and business-to-business collaborations, as networks between large and small business are almost non-existent. The funding issue could be eased if poorly designed government regulations changed to the benefit of small businesses, and large companies and multinationals would certainly benefit from the flexibility of entrepreneurial thinking. By embracing the entrepreneurial way of doing business (creating, prototyping, succeeding or failing, learning and doing it all over again) the innovation process would be a lot more cost effective. If I could advise on how to foster the entrepreneurial spirit among young people I would suggest establishing societies within universities, creating stronger media platforms where people could exchange ideas and experiences and holding events on a regular basis in order to forge partnerships and ventures.

Just like running, the road less travelled is not for everybody, but those that do want to travel it should be encouraged to do so . . .

7
Bottletop, UK

Oliver Wayman and Cameron Saul
Company founders and directors

Bottletop sets out to redefine the concept of 'Luxury' through collections that celebrate true craftsmanship, rediscover hidden production techniques and form a timeless 'created by hand' aesthetic; designs that are an object of both pride and beauty for the artisan and consumer alike. We place the importance of the design and finish alongside the quality of the production process itself; the way in which the artisan has been trained and supported to create each stitch and every weave.

Behind all Bottletop creative processes is a mission and commitment to empower women with livelihoods and young people with education. It also today funds the operation of the Bottletop Foundation, enabling all funds raised through music and contemporary art projects to support life-changing education projects for young people.

Even though the mission has remained consistent throughout, it has been through a variety of structures and product ranges over time. Over this chapter we aim to tell you a brief history of how it all came about.

Cameron Saul:

I started the Bottletop Foundation charity in 2002. I arrived in a remote village in Uganda to teach teenagers how to protect themselves from HIV/AIDS. I found myself in classrooms with more than a hundred students who could barely speak English, in a culture where sex and HIV is shrouded in secrecy and taboo, thinking 'how can we possibly help these youngsters to protect themselves!' I nearly gave up before we began.

Six months later those same students staged one of the most important days in the history of that village; a health day. They took over from us and taught their friends and family about HIV as well as gender inequality, substance abuse and the dangers of teenage pregnancy through drama, songs, debate and all in their local, tribal tongue. That day I learned an important lesson. Young people can be empowered to protect themselves and their friends, families and wider communities through the right creative health education.

I discovered a handbag made from recycled bottle tops by artisans in Kenya and lined it with beautiful leather from Mulberry which was my father's company. The bag became the best selling bag of the season for Mulberry and generated the most press they had received for any campaign as well as raising major funds for education projects.

Oliver Wayman:

My story began in 2002. Fresh out of school I decided to embark on a trip to Ghana to work in a radio station. I didn't want to go straight to full-time work/university so I saved some money from working in a call centre and started to look into the possibilities which were available for working abroad in more unusual places. I wanted to see somewhere different and not just travel for the sake of travelling but really immerse myself in a different culture. There were plenty of teaching jobs but I found a job at a Ghanaian radio station which I found much more appealing. I went out there quite naively, not really knowing what to expect. I came back having felt truly inspired by the place and the wonderful people but also struck by the poverty which was prevalent throughout the country. Unfortunately that also left me feeling a bit helpless. I didn't really know what I could do to help the problem, but it did leave me with a very strong sentiment to do more, that I knew I wanted to revisit after further studies.

I came back to the UK and completed a degree in International Relations at Sussex University. I had always had a desire to work in the music industry and while studying I managed to land myself the position of a talent scout looking for new bands. I actually felt this was the natural path I was going to take. I had been lucky enough to forward some successful bands at an early stage and felt I would continue in this area. I met Cameron at an electronic music night in Brighton through mutual friends and he mentioned he needed a bit of help on a new album series he was putting together to raise money for the foundation. I volunteered for a while and helped release the record. Unfortunately it was at the height of a very large transition in the music industry in which young people were no longer buying much music, so fundraising for the foundation through record sales was becoming an increasingly difficult task. We did still manage to raise a bit through our own club nights with famous DJs which helped to keep everything running. Cameron was tired and needed a change of scenery; he was keen to close the foundation down but didn't because one of the team, Jono Pattinson, was very keen to keep it running. I continued to work for both the record label and the charity, working on a follow-up Brazilian influenced record. The charity was staying afloat but not really raising enough funds to justify its existence. The fundraising was predominantly being generated by Cameron's father's events in Somerset and he, too, was tiring of keeping the thing going.

There was however a new discovery which was beginning to make me explore a new production technique. My mother had showed me an incredible bag which she had come across at a market which originated in Brazil. A beautiful, silver, chain mail-like mesh: tactile and chic. Even more interesting for me was that it was made entirely from upcycled aluminium ring pulls. You would never realise the waste material it was made from by looking at the product, which in fact was its strength.

Cameron had had great success with his pop art Bottletop bag a few years before and I felt it could be a great progression for the trading side of the charity. I started researching different cooperative groups and even approached the Brazilian embassy to help me to source a group which could produce using this intricate crocheting technique. There were many but unfortunately not any producing any products of real quality. I felt frustrated, as I couldn't seem to find a project that could make this work. However, Cameron and I had picked up a few sample bags while on holiday in a market in Salvador, so we knew the groups existed.

The 'game changing' moment came when I approached the record label, Mr Bongo, which we had worked with on the Brazilian album, to help me find the right producers. David, the label owner, introduced me on Skype to a guy called Luciano Dos Santos. He was an ex-favela resident running a local charity which David was supporting. Luciano was an inspiration; he had a good grasp of English as he had been in foster care in Canada for two years having charmed his way into the family of a Canadian couple who he was trying to sell snacks to on the beach in Brazil. He was motivated, dynamic, had a business approach to work but also a real heart of gold. He sourced a cooperative straight away and sent me a batch of bags a week later. I still remember opening that first box and praying that they would be the correct ones. Fortunately, they were. We sold them as merchandise for the launch of the Brazilian record and there was a huge demand on the night. We were on to something special.

Cameron rejoined the foundation and we began working with a British clothing brand to help distribute the product. We were doing reasonable volumes and were genuinely excited about the potential in the product. We went back to visit the cooperative with Luciano and were really impressed by the set-up. Our Portuguese was limited and the woman who ran the cooperative didn't speak any English so it was hard to get a full understanding of the specifics of the operation. Luciano took two of the mobile telephone numbers of the workers in secret as we wanted to do our due diligence and we weren't getting precise information on the workers' salaries. The information which Luciano discovered was very disappointing: the workers weren't receiving a fair wage and we felt that the woman running the cooperative was taking the lion's share of the profit.

We had a dilemma; we had a beautifully made product made from upcycled materials but produced with questionable ethics. Luciano and I had many long Skype conversations deciding the next best course of action, and stopping the production was a very real possibility. We decided on a DIY approach which became the foundations of the project we have today. Luciano made it clear that unemployment was rife in his community and we thought we could transfer a lot of the skills into his own community. We invited the women who Luciano had befriended from the other cooperative and paid them to give free lessons to the women from Luciano's community. We purchased all the raw materials, including used ring pulls from waste collectors. The class was open to all residents from the community and the first session had just eight people. We were a little disappointed with the turnout but decided to persist and see how they coped with learning the crocheting technique. Three dropped out, but the remaining five excelled. They were making perfectly produced belts within one month and the first 'Bellani' (Oliver's mother's maiden name) bags within two.

Around this time we brought the DJ Fatboy Slim to visit the project in Brazil. He lived where our office was based in Brighton and is a huge artist in Brazil. He had recently attracted more people than the

Rolling Stones at a beach party in Rio with over a million spectators! We took out a journalist who wrote a fantastic feature for a British national newspaper which came at a critical time for the charity. Cameron had managed to secure a grant to cover six months of running costs and we decided we would give it our best shot and see whether we could increase our fundraising.

Fortunately we did. The trading company of the charity made a profit and we raised more money in donations than we ever had before. Cameron launched our Full Circle annual art fundraiser at the Roundhouse in London to great acclaim. This cemented the organisation into the art world thanks to commissioned pieces from the likes of the Turner Prize winner Rachel Whiteread. We were now in a position to try to grow the charity and for the first time were able to start formulating longer-term strategies and new approaches.

Part of this strategy was to restructure the organisation. We had been advised by Pauline Broomhead at the Forum for Social Improvement that, due to the success of the trading company, we would in fact be better suited to moving the fashion side over to a new social enterprise. We would still retain a solid link to the foundation and continue the social mission of poverty alleviation and youth empowerment. All of the foundation's running costs would be removed and it would be in the very enviable position from a small charity's perspective of saying that all the donations made would go straight to the beneficiary projects.

We realised we needed to raise capital to invest in business areas such as production, marketing and PR and had no intention of allocating donor money to this. Social investment was needed and we began doing the rounds of previous supporters of the charity and seeing if they would be interested in supporting us. We managed to close our first friends and family round of funding in 2011.

This changed everything for us. We now had the liquidity to refine production and work on new, exciting designs. We invited Iain Renwick, the ex-CEO of Liberty department stores, to be chairman and he made an introduction to Atelier du Sartel, headed by Vincent du Sartel, the ex-head of accessory design for Louis Vuitton and creative director at Loewe. He and his team created a stunning set of designs and formed a whole new production process which moved the collection on significantly. There was now an intricate leather braiding technique in which the ring pulls were woven in between the leather strands, which gave the designs a whole new aesthetic.

We began by flying out one of Vincent's team, Clara Camus, to the project to help train the team in the favela in these complex techniques. It took a lot of refining but over time we were able to perfect the technique.

We now found that we had a very credible fashion offering which didn't look out of place on the shelves of some of the finest department stores in the world. It has been a long journey, but one which we hope we can continue to grow and replicate in new geographies and, in doing so, employing more people in developing communities and providing more life-changing education for young people through the Bottletop Foundation.

8

Big Blue Bike, USA

Shudhan Kohli
Company founder and director

My forefathers were indentured servants from India who came to East Africa with the British to develop the railway that now spans from north to south of Kenya. When the country won its independence, the immigrant Indian population found themselves in limbo as they were no longer recognised as Indians by their native land and locals considered them symbols of the country's colonial past. With few resources and a strong will to succeed, the group's entrepreneurial spirit was the primary driver of the region's growth and innovation which eventually saw them become the cornerstone of East Africa's economy.

I was raised in and among this group of businessmen. My grandfather was one of the most respected businessmen in western Kenya, known for successfully running a multitude of businesses in industries ranging from gourmet foods to construction materials. By the time I was born in the mid-1980s, he was in the last few years of his life with his assets on a downward spiral due to bad management. As I grew up, I began to realise his name was of a legendary status in my town, for reasons beyond the business exploits he was known for. I would regularly encounter people whose lives he had touched with his philanthropy. His contribution to the community around him left a mark that stayed around for years after his death. His name gave my family special status at the local market for discounted rate produce and a reserved spot at the front of every line as it was very likely that it was his support decades ago that allowed the vendors to set up shop in the first place. As I grew up, I began to realise what a tough act it would be to emulate the business and philanthropic endeavours of my paternal grandfather. With time, I realised the true weight on my shoulders when I learned that my maternal grandfather had an equally iconic status as a figurehead and leading community organiser in India's peaceful fight for independence from the British. I would hear stories of his efforts to improve women's rights and abolish the caste system that still plagues India today. For his time, he was a true visionary and a decorated symbol of progressive values. My grandfathers' legacies helped lay out my path to becoming a social entrepreneur, striving to create businesses that deliver profits to shareholders while providing a sustainable and positive impact on impoverished communities and the environment.

Graduating with a bachelor's degree in economics from the University of Texas at Austin, I had a job as a management consultant lined up to start almost immediately after graduation. I knew this would probably be the only time I had in my life to travel and open myself up to new cultures, so I turned in a request to push my start date eight months forward. Peru happened to be the cheapest country to fly to in South America and little did I know that this would be the country that would be instrumental in inspiring my start-up idea and the primary mission for the rest of my 20s. Traveling through Peru, I noticed the abundance of exceptionally high quality fibres and textiles—from pima cotton to baby alpaca—that truly deserved the luxury status attributed to them. I was ignorant about textiles and apparel at the time and had never heard of either of those products, but I was fairly sure there wasn't enough of it being marketed in North America. With this in mind, the rest of my journey through South America lasted another four months, during which I became immersed in the Latin culture, people and language, aspects that would be invaluable for the business I was eventually going to start.

Months went by and I started a new life in Los Angeles in a high-powered consulting position and fully immersed in the corporate lifestyle. This, without mentioning the perks of being in a city that provided all the extravagances and nightlife a young bachelor would enjoy. Despite this, I kept growing restless as the entrepreneur within me wanted to create something that was groundbreaking and disruptive. Weekends that were typically spent nursing hangovers soon became intense research sessions in coffee shops as I began to embrace the idea of importing the baby alpaca fibre I encountered while in Peru. The concept was simple. Import knitwear made using baby alpaca fibre and market it as an exquisite and unique material to high-end stores. Alpaca was being sold in the US, but the premium version of the fibre was scarcely found and certainly had room for market entrants. Despite this, the more I researched the feasibility of the business idea, the more I realised the strong foothold cashmere had in the space. Cashmere is a brand in its own right that symbolises premium quality knits. Competing with this well-established recognition was going to be a gargantuan task and I realised I had to find a niche if I ever wanted to grab any sort of market share with baby alpaca products. While attempting to understand the primary differences between the two rival materials, I stumbled upon research about the eco-friendly nature of alpacas, which greatly differed from the destructive grazing habits of cashmere goats in Asia. Uncovering this truth set off the domino effect that eventually led to the Big Blue Bike.

Alpacas are hardy animals that require very little water and land resources in order to sustain themselves. Their padded hooves do not tear up the earth beneath them and scissor-like teeth trim the grass they feed on rather than completely uproot it. What's more, the faecal matter of these remarkable animals is a source of biofuel for herding communities. In stark contrast, cashmere goats require large amounts of water and land to graze on. Their stiletto-like hooves rip the ground under them and they uproot plants that they graze on. The combination of these characteristics causes soil erosion which, in conjunction with their excessive water requirements, has caused deserts to develop in what used to be vast grasslands in inner-Mongolia. Demand for cashmere has led to an overpopulation of the goats with no hope for change unless there is a dramatic shift in consumption patterns. I saw the potential of displacing this environmental strain by marketing an alternative that maintained the quality and luxurious attributes of cashmere while being friendlier to the environment.

So there I was with a business solution that had the potential to impact positively on an environmental crisis. The next question in my mind was whether there was a business within this solution. Answering this question led me to the growing eco-fashion movement that was making ripples in the industry. Consumers were beginning to see the environmental and social toll of their apparel purchases. Toxic materials and unethical labour practices are rampant in the industry and conscious consumers were beginning to vote with their dollars for brands that would address their concerns. Encouraged by this fast-growing movement and the unique product I could provide, I found myself devoting more and more time to the endeavour while shifting the focus away from my corporate career. When I decided the time was right to take the plunge, within a matter of days I found myself without my company-provided apartment and car or the security of a regular pay cheque. As I began to settle into a new life on my friend's couch, I found myself confronting an industry in which I had neither experience nor any contacts. I spent the first few weeks trying to familiarise myself with the fashion world. With some smarts I managed to convince a trade show organiser that I was a buyer from London, giving me a free pass to the event. Here, I soaked in everything I could about the industry. I got my hands on catalogues and line sheets while watching industry pros pitching their wares. It was my first glance into the industry's inner workings and the closely knit community that it is so known for. The event gave me some contacts for buyers in the area who I reached out to for advice. They became great resources of information and provided me with the market insight I needed as I developed the model of my start-up.

First, I had to decide between having a wholesale or a retail model. I knew that the huge investment in inventory that would be required in a retail setting would pose a high risk for the business. In addition, as a start-up with very limited resources, dealing with a large customer base and maintaining the level of service required for a successful B2C operation would be quite a tremendous strain to a small business. Adopting a wholesale model would counter both of these challenges. Once a set of samples were developed, I would be allowed to gather orders in larger quantities and produce only that which is sold—effectively eliminating the risk involved in inventory investments. Second, as a one-man show, it was a lot more realistic to deal with a handful of wholesale accounts than interacting with and fulfilling obligations to multiple customers. Once a wholesale model was determined to be the best option to move forward with, I began to explore who my target would be. I dabbled with the idea of supplying to sustainable brands looking to expand their product offering or creating a brand and marketing directly to stores and boutiques. Both options had their pros and cons; however, I recognised the importance of having a strong brand with a loyal following as a barrier for new market entrants. The sustainable apparel space still did not have a dominant brand that represented the movement. The ones that did have a strong presence were providing apparel for the outdoor and active lifestyles, a product very different from what I envisioned. It made sense to create a brand that could one day expand to other product verticals that maintained high quality and design standards for the conscious consumer.

My first trip to Peru was filled with uncertainty. I did not have a single contact in the country and my Spanish was merely basic. I contacted the Peruvian consulate in Los Angeles for a list of reliable knitwear manufacturers who I proceeded to set appointments with during the first two weeks of my trip to the country. I understood that I had very limited savings that would have to pay for my personal expenses while serving as seed capital for my new venture. Checking into a hostel dorm, I spent the next two months visiting the various players in the supply chain and diving into the technicalities of the production process. Design was of utmost importance as it was going to be a primary differentiator of the brand, so I contacted all the design schools in Lima in an effort to recruit their best students to join the project. I learned about the production methods by visiting multiple knitwear manufacturers while also mingling with material providers to learn about pricing, supply and turnaround times of the alpaca fibre itself.

The investigative process led me to NGOs that train women in impoverished regions of Peru in knitting methods with the goal of providing them with an income stream to support their families while being able to work from home as they tend their children. I instantly saw the opportunity to add a social component to the apparel and was excited about the prospect of eventually sourcing the knitwear from these women, positively impacting their income. As I analysed the women's production capability, I quickly realised that they were lacking in quality control and design know-how, which would pose a significant hurdle down the road. This did not deter me as I saw my project as an opportunity to get the women's products up to par, allowing them access to international markets in the future. The social component of the brand had to be put on hold as I still had to test the market with a quality product meeting the promises of the brand. I eventually partnered with a medium-sized knitwear manufacturer that was involved in the export of alpaca knitwear to Europe and the rest of South America and was recognised by the Peruvian Government for its high standards in ethical business practices. Working with them in the design and production of the Big Blue Bike's first collection gave me the security of knowing my production was being handled by experienced professionals that knew the importance of quality control and had the ability to meet strict deadlines. The added benefit was the insider knowledge I got in manufacturing best practices that I would take with me when I would eventually begin partnering with small, women-owned businesses and cooperatives.

I approached the first collection knowing that it was going to unearth information that would eventually determine the direction of the Big Blue Bike. This led me to add as much variety to the collection as possible by making designs that were classic and 'safe' to those that were more contemporary. The entire collection was a collage of different knitting styles that varied greatly in price points. To further test the waters, I made a small men's collection and a line of hand-knit designs (in addition to the ones that were made using manually operated looms). By April 2010, four months after I landed in Peru, I had completed the collection and wrapped up my first photoshoot having recruited my models in the hostel I was staying in and at a shopping mall—one of many ways I had found to cut costs for the bootstrapped venture!

In fashion, the buying season for winter collections lasts from January to March of each year. I was arriving in the US to begin my sales in April and was well aware of the disadvantage I was going to have. It was either selling the collection late or waiting until the following buying season—in a year's time. Feeling fairly comfortable with my knowledge of the production and design processes and having leveraged the contacts I made in Los Angeles to develop my catalogue and marketing material, I realised that I had only worked on 50% of the business, with a massive gap left in distribution and marketing. I had no sales plan, besides copying and pasting names and contact information for stores my competitors were selling to onto an Excel sheet. I moved back in with my parents and out of my bedroom I spent countless hours emailing and cold calling to generate sales for the collection I had worked so hard for. I easily worked 14-hour days, making an average of 70 phone calls a day and sending out hundreds of emails. Both my wrists had to be bandaged to prevent any long-term damage from the hours I spent in front of my laptop. Success was hard to achieve. The US was in the middle of a recession and the fashion industry is known to be the most sensitive in an economic downturn, while being the last to catch up during a recovery. Despite this, I managed to set appointments with some Californian boutiques and took the next flight out to present the collection. Sleeping on friends' couches, I moved from city to city presenting my collection to the boutiques, and the response was overwhelming. Every buyer that interacted with the product, bought. They were sold on the feel of the material and the designs. The sales process was the best opportunity I had to gain important market information. I probed the buyers on product features they would like to see as well as price points and brand positioning. Armed with a set of purchase orders, I returned to Peru feeling triumphant after a relatively successful pilot stage. I had gained vital information on design, pricing and other aspects that would allow me to approach the next collection with a more knowledgeable perspective.

Before putting any thought to the next steps in marketing and development of a new collection, I had to put my complete focus on fulfilling the purchase orders with a 0% defect rate and an on-time delivery. Unfortunately, as much as a business can be planned to perfection, it is going to have to rely on its ecosystem for successful execution. The business environment in Peru is filled with uncertainties. Deadlines are always flexible and contracts hardly ever enforced. Functioning as the 'little guy' makes this even more difficult as production and material suppliers can lose you as a customer without ever noticing. It was this harsh reality that I faced when I returned to Peru to oversee production of the collection I had just sold.

The alpaca industry is dominated by two powerful players who have a stranglehold on the entire supply chain. That year, they prioritised exports of their fibre to Europe and China, instead of supplying domestic manufacturers. This caused delays in accessing the material and long waitlists for anyone hoping to get a hold of the material.

Putting the situation in positive light for my buyers, I promptly gave them the good news that they would be among the exclusive few US boutiques that would have access to the premium material, though it would be arriving a little later than projected.

With production running over one-and-a-half months behind schedule, I saw the industry's reliance on the duopoly as a major threat to my business. As I began digging into the alpaca fibre trade and analysing the supply chain, I began to meet herding communities and intermediaries in the process. I came across a problem I had encountered years before as I travelled through Peru as a backpacker. I revisited the discovery that there was a disproportionate demand for white alpacas due to the relative ease in applying chemical dyes on the non-coloured fibre. This has led herding communities to selectively breed out coloured animals, causing a worrying imbalance in the biodiversity of the species. I realised that businesses like mine could help reverse this cycle and positively impact on the animal's population by specifically demanding naturally coloured yarn. My investigations also revealed that the process of turning the raw fibre into ready-to-knit yarn was a complex operation with closely kept industry secrets and expensive machinery, and a bureaucratic process that was designed to specifically hinder any new entrants in the market. I found that most margins in the chain were being made by intermediaries and the companies involved in the manufacturing of the yarn—with barely anything paid to herding communities. I found that even a small amount of knowledge on the part of the herders—such as being able to sort between the qualities of their material—would triple the value of their products and consequently their income. Even if we were unable to assist the herding communities to fully convert their raw fibre to yarn, there was an easy solution to boosting their income in the short term. Partnering with a local NGO, I proceeded to meet rural mountain communities with the eventual goal of training and adding value to their wares to increase their participation in the multi-million dollar alpaca fibre supply chain.

As time went along, production was nearing completion and I had given notice to all my buyers to expect delivery of their merchandise. Little did I know that there was another surprise in the works. The intricately made sweaters were carefully folded and packed away in boxes ready for an expedited air shipment to the US when I realised that delivery confirmations were not coming through from the carrier. Having tried for two days to access the information, I reached out to my manufacturers who were responsible for the safe and timely delivery of the merchandise. It turned out that the boxes were placed on the wrong delivery truck and after two panic-filled and stressful weeks, the items were found to be sitting and left unclaimed at a truck stop in a desert in northern Peru. This was another testament of the unpredictable environment social entrepreneurs do business in.

The eventual delivery of the orders saw much-needed revenue for the company. A new collection was developed, refined using lessons learned from the first production cycle. A new wave of sales calls was waiting to happen. I recognised the limitations of running sales out of my bedroom. A lack of funds made it impossible for me to access buyers at trade shows and due to the nature of the business, buyers make purchase decisions after physically seeing and interacting with the products. Being able to afford one set of samples made the effort even more challenging. The second collection was met with an even more overwhelming response; however, red flags of a declining industry were everywhere. Buyers were asking for extended credit and half the boutiques I had sold to previously had gone out of business. Despite this, and my limitation in sales capabilities, I managed to marginally increase the company's revenue from the previous year.

The plan was to complete the second round of sales and partner with a sales agency to head a more thorough sales process the next time around while seeking funding as the project wrapped up the pilot phase and began a full-fledged implementation. The cyclical nature of the fashion industry was beginning to cause a severe strain on the company's cash flow. Income only came at the end of each year when winter deliveries were made. In order to cut costs, I trusted my manufacturing partners to oversee production on their own without my presence in the country and decided to reintroduce the same collection from the previous year. By now, I had a healthy network of contacts in the fashion industry and was subsequently introduced to an agency that I eventually contracted to head sales for the following buying season. Over the same time period, with some good fortune, the company was taken on by an incubator of social businesses that provided me with the expertise and know-how that helped lay out the strategic framework for the full-fledged implementation phase of the project. Through the incubator, I managed to assemble a highly qualified board of advisers who ranged in skills from marketing to implementation of development projects. I spent the entire year in 2011 closely working with the incubator laying out the strategic framework for scaled production and marketing. Strategising and theorising on paper is one thing but undertaking a full-fledged implementation is a whole other proposition that requires financial and human resources—both of which I was short in. Finding an angel investor became absolutely critical to maintaining and growing the business. The search for funding while maintaining company operations singlehandedly is a gargantuan task that will lead even the strongest willed to a complete burnout. Twelve-hour workdays became the norm and it would be safe to say that I had become a hermit with no life outside of the Big Blue Bike. I was fortunate enough to have a girlfriend who understood my commitment to the business and was supportive of my efforts. Her presence in my life gave me the balance I needed and an opportunity for much needed rejuvenation of my mental processes.

As the year came to a close, delivery for 2011's winter collection was made safely and on time, without the upheaval of the previous year. As sales were being handled by the agency I had recently partnered with, I had the freedom to focus my attention on production and fully implement the social business. I arrived in Lima in February 2012 without anticipating the roller-coaster year ahead of me.

As the showroom in Los Angeles headed sales efforts, I began the process of meeting and interviewing women's groups and cooperatives with the goal to partner with one that would allow us to deliver the positive social impact we sought to provide. The intense search led me to the southern Peruvian city of Arequipa where I met a female entrepreneur with physical assets required to produce the knitwear we needed while being located in an underemployed and low-income neighbourhood. At this time, sales figures were beginning to trickle in from the showroom in Los Angeles and it did not look good. The numbers were marginally better than the previous year; however, not enough to justify the added expense of hiring the agency. The reason cited was that buyers were not taking risks by investing in untested brands in an uncertain market. To sustain the company's operations, I knew I had to develop a spring collection for an additional round of revenue. Alpaca is a lightweight material that can be airy and cool when knit correctly and would be a perfect material for spring knits. The sales agency strongly insisted that I did not create a collection for the spring using alpaca because of its general perception as a winter product. They admitted that consumers would be more open to purchasing alpaca for a light and airy knit during the spring; however, the rigid and backward mentality of fashion buyers would prevent their acceptance of the material in warmer months. Working with the sales agency further revealed the nature of the industry. Their insistence on filling out paper orders in an age when digitised information was increasing efficiency was frustrating. Monthly payments were only accepted in the form of a physical cheque and having them scan receipts and purchase orders for email delivery was a challenge in itself. Buyers were unwilling to pay for their orders with their credit cards on a secure online checkout page, and insisted on a phone call to process orders—a requirement that caused quite a lot of inconvenience when having to work out of a remote region of Peru with unreliable phone connectivity and the difficulty in getting buyers on the phone during their workday.

My experiences in this industry showed me the importance of reaching out to and selling directly to consumers. This first revelation would determine things to come; however, I had to take what I had and build on it before completely pivoting my model. I received an ultimatum from my sales showroom that if I did not use a material other than alpaca for the spring, they would drop the line—putting the company at a massive risk. They were our only hope for entry into new US markets. I rationalised that they knew the market better than anyone else would and were respected figureheads in the Los Angeles fashion scene. The job of any entrepreneur is to listen to the market and provide what it wants, and so I proceeded to research organic pima cotton coloured using organic dyes made from vegetable and plant extracts as an alternative spring material. It made complete sense to me. Pima cotton is one of the finest cottons in the world and when certified organic, the level of quality improves while making it an eco-friendly product. The dying process would provide a unique and innovative product that would suit the high end and sustainable consumer. Market research showed that eco-fashion was continuing to grow along with the demand for organic cotton; however, there was nobody in the space providing organic pima cotton, let alone a naturally dyed product. My sales partners in Los Angeles gave the thumbs up and I proceeded with the time-intensive process of prototyping tints with a natural dying facility while overseeing sample development of designs using the organic material. I hedged my risks by actively involving the head of the sales agency in the design and prototype process and only proceeded with her approval. I was simultaneously seeking investors and was invited to present the business at a conference in Mexico pertaining to Impact Investing, a new field of investing targeted towards socially and environmentally impacting businesses. Considered a pioneering entrepreneur in South America within this field, I was also invited to present to Chilean and Peruvian angel groups—both yielding strategic contacts rather than financial partners, one of whom happened to be among South

America's leading fashion designers who I would eventually work with later in the year.

With another new collection completed, this time using a revolutionary material and dying process, the collection was shipped to Los Angeles ready for spring sales. As the sales season unfolded, I was greeted with a pleasant surprise that the Big Blue Bike was selected among the top five businesses in emerging markets, out of 300 entrants, by a prominent investor network. I was given the opportunity to present and network at a conference in The Hague and it was one night before my presentation to investors that I got notification that we had been dropped by the sales agency in Los Angeles citing low sales of the new collection. The time, effort and financial resources I had put into researching and developing a whole new line of products for the spring had been thrown out of the window and I was facing the prospect of not seeing any new revenue till the following year.

Despite the setback, I proceeded with the presentation and once again failed to attract an investor. The company's cash reserves were worn down to the bone and with no sales channels nor any financial backing, I was on the verge of cutting my losses and wrapping up the project. As has always been the case ever since I began working on the Big Blue Bike, when one door slammed shut, another opened. The conference in The Hague led to a meeting with a high profile fashion distributor in Amsterdam which was enthusiastic about the brand and its products. Following intense negotiations, with an experienced board member beside me—a contact I had made during the conference who has been a close mentor ever since—we agreed to sign an exclusive agreement with the firm who promised to boost revenues tenfold while distributing the product across Europe. This was the kind of break every entrepreneur dreams of. The only caveat was that I had to adapt the product to a lower price point in order to match up to the realities of the European market at the time. According to the distributors, consumers purchasing luxury products would only consider brands they recognised and trusted. For any new brand entering the fray, its status would have to appeal to the mid-range market commanding lower price points.

I returned to Peru with a monumental task at hand. I had to, once again, recreate a product to fit their rigid pricing structure while designing a collection double the size I was typically used to within two months. Having already worked closely with the woman-owned enterprise in southern Peru for the failed spring collection, I was aware of their capabilities (or lack thereof). I brought on board the award-winning South American fashion designer, mentioned earlier, and offered the prospect of eventually becoming an equity-wielding partner dependent on the success of this collection. We moved away from the premium alpaca material we normally used and switched to a lower quality version of the fibre and used material blends that were both sustainable and would bring down the costs of production. The designer's involvement helped distribute the workload which would certainly have been beyond my means. Getting the collection completed on time required the mother of all scrambles. Four days before the trade show in Amsterdam, I had a camera crew and model working overnight at a makeshift studio in my apartment in Peru. After every successful shot of the piece, I would hand it over to my friend who waited with a needle and thread to sew on the logo and washing instructions before folding and packing the item in a box. The photoshoot was followed by a dash to the airport at dawn for the next flight to Lima to deliver the collection to a courier in time for the next plane out to Amsterdam. The boxes managed to arrive hours before the trade show started and we all breathed a collective sigh of relief, eager to hear the results of our efforts.

Once again, disappointment awaited. Orders were low and would not justify a production run. The distributors blamed the economy; however, I was not willing to accept any excuses. I had spent an entire year in Peru creating two collections that did not yield any returns. I found myself deep in debt and returned to the US dejected. I had sacrificed a relationship and my entire personal life to create something that had ultimately failed. I took a break from the business to decide on how to move forward while contemplating what could have been done differently. I remained confident about my product; however, the two events that promised to grow the company—partnerships with the sales showroom in LA and distributors in Europe—required me to divert away from my core competence, which was premium quality alpaca with versatile and wearable designs. I should have been wary of having to adapt my product and market to meet the needs of my contracted sales partners. I thought I was doing what every entrepreneur is expected to do and that is to listen to the market; however, in the process I lost focus of who the market truly was and left the direction of the company in the hands of others. In the US, I saw signs of an industry that was not only in the middle of a downward spiral but one that was fundamentally backward and reliant on a handful of buyers that would determine the success and failure of brands. Having a presence in a large trade show would expose any clothing line to a multitude of buying prospects, but the exorbitant price to present at these exhibitions would be prohibitive for any upcoming brand. I began to recognise that consumers would be more willing to embrace a brand that disrupted the common notion of fashion far more than the establishment that runs the industry. The irony is that fashion is one of the most innovation-driven industries, with the requirement to adapt constantly while keeping a close pulse on trends. This dedication to groundbreaking designs is not translated to the way the industry fundamentally functions; however, we are in the early beginnings of the digitisation of the industry. Entrepreneurs are beginning to bring networks of fashion sales reps and wholesale buyers to the online world with collection viewings held on virtual trade shows. This should eventually see a more cost-efficient and streamlined business process favourable to brands without the network of contacts and financial clout to penetrate the industry.

The confidence in my product still holds; however, there needs to be a fundamental shift in the business's model. In order to counter the cyclical nature of the fashion industry's buying seasons, which causes a massive strain in cash flow, I am in the process of pivoting to a retail model that promises constant and year-round sales. By conducting sales online, marketing efforts can be tracked on a real-time basis allowing for more educated investments. Importantly, customer acquisition costs can be kept low as there is no need for expensive tradeshows and sales agents to gain access to the market. Functioning in a retail environment does have its own operational drawbacks. Managing a larger number of clients requires the setup of a customer service team and the need for regular stock which can be both risky and cash intensive. The Big Blue Bike has been a collection of successes and failures and I've found that every series of failures leads to a success that creates a milestone for the company and a foot forward. I am eager to experience the next milestone on the journey of the company that has been a part of me for most of my 20s.

9

Estancia Peuma Hue, Argentina

Evelyn Hoter
Company founder and director

The seeds that made it possible

I was seven years old and I told my mom: 'When I grow up, I will live in Bariloche'. Originally from Buenos Aires, Argentina, my family and I had been skiing in Bariloche (main gateway to North Patagonia) every year since I was three. The project at Peuma Hue has its roots way back in my childhood—or even before? Nature in general and particularly mountains have always been a strong pull in my life; and I understand my grandfather, who sadly passed away before I was born, shared the same passion. In my free art classes at school, all I could draw was a place exactly like Peuma Hue. When I was 17—by then already going on my own to the mountains when I had some free time—I was doing well in my last year at high school, so I asked my mom if she would allow me to stay in the mountains and quit school for some weeks. I just couldn't return! I stayed more than a month and when back at school, couldn't think about anything other than the creeks and mountains, forest and waterfalls. When I turned 21, I graduated in psychology and finally moved to Bariloche. I started my practice as a psychotherapist; I was finally living where my heart belonged.

Life and hazards forced me to go back to Buenos Aires at age 28, grieving. I had to come back and visit my heart left behind in those ranges and with my friends; so while in BA, I kept coming back to Bariloche four times a year! After 24 years of being a psychotherapist and then a life coach, I needed something different. Having been drawn by the outdoors and active sports since I was very young, I moved to something different and co-owned a nature and adventure travel agency for four years, thus learning the basis of the tourist business and organising for others what I so much loved for myself. Unknowingly, my life was going through all the different stages and learning I needed to approach the 'Peuma Hue project'. Having been gifted by the opportunity to travel throughout my life as well, I had learned a lot about service and tourism from the client's point of view.

Life went on. After a first divorce, I then remarried and when planning to retire with my second husband, we started to look for a place to buy in Bariloche. The moment I stepped on Peuma Hue's grounds I had the most significant and clear certainty in my life: I had finally reached 'home'. Before this, I could have lived in many places; I did not feel really grounded anywhere. Hard to describe, people ask me if it was a 'vision'. I had no vision, it was a body feeling: I felt drawn and pulled by the ground below my feet; I was certain this was home for me. At that time, Peuma Hue was 500 acres of National Park land by a lake and at the foot of a mountain we later found out was the steepest vertical drop in the area. Standing by the crystal clear blue-green lake, we were surrounded by pristine forest, jagged peaks on one side, rolling hills of an older mountain fold on the other. Behind, we couldn't see much. It was completely undiscovered, abandoned and almost impenetrable, extremely depredated; the invasive introduced rosehip had taken over where the forest had been previously chopped down and local cattle, illegal felling and poaching aggravated it further. We could barely move into the thickness, nothing was in sight unless we were on the lakeshore. But I couldn't move—literally! I couldn't leave!! It took us a year and a half until we were able to buy it. All the efforts of providing me with alternatives in the meantime were useless. This was where I wanted to be.

I was brought up in a family who was used to a very high-quality lifestyle. High standards are ingrained in me. For me, 'luxury' has to do with non-pretentious, high-quality service. And this is the essence of everything we offer: from our cosy and elegant-rustic style, that blends wood and antiques, to our gourmet meals that are not only delicious, balanced, healthy and based on our organic garden but also served with care and design in my grandmother's exquisite china and silver. We offer activities in this amazingly majestic nature; our horse guide is not only a guide, she's the best horse-whisperer and animal communicator I know. We have a hostess who not only introduces Peuma Hue to our guests and organises all the services and their activities with detail; but her genuine passion for the place, her smile and love for animals, is contagious. And we offer massages, where our masseur not only blends several techniques but has a way of focusing and 'knowing' your body that results in what most of our guests refer to as their 'best massage' ever. Our gardener has 'eagle eyes' that allowed him to preserve every single little tree of the native forest when cutting the invasive rosehip and manages our garden in a way that only one endeared to the land can do. The thoughtful, caring and professional attitude of our sales person enhances our guests' stay. And we have a dedicated and thoughtful manager who, besides dealing with tons of different aspects with expertise and never losing his temper, achieves the most wonderful spirit in our team, leading and motivating them into a common goal. And I could go on and on, referring to the warmth and high quality of each one in our team, where every single person has a special charm and human values that make them unique in what they do. And we have the loving attitude of our animals—among themselves and with guests—some guests referring to them as being in paradise, puzzled by the harmony between those that naturally should be chasing, fighting or threatening each other in some way. So this is 'luxury' for us; it is the best quality we can offer in what we offer.

And then there is 'sustainability'. What are we without being balanced with what surrounds us through time? We are in a very special moment in the history of our planet that shows in an overwhelming way and with more clearness than ever before, the devastating effects of the careless doing of humankind. Having been blessed by intelligence and lots of creativity, we disconnected from being in balance among ourselves and with the rest of the planet. We came up with lineal paradigms of everlasting growth, abuse and extraction that are absolutely unsustainable in a finite planet. We at Peuma Hue live in a paradise of beauty, clean waters that are still safe to drink from their sources, pristine forests that host a number of varieties of plant and animal life. I want this to be enjoyed for generations to come, so whatever we wish to offer and open to others needs to be within this understanding. And this leads to moderation, to the essence of what is valuable, to thoughtfulness, consciousness and education.

So, based on these principles, we started, step by step, in a land that at that time was far from being looked after. It was depredated and invaded. It took extremely hard work; consuming 100% of my life and that of many others, tons of love and commitment, facing different fears and challenges all these years. We started from scratch; clearing part of the land from the invasive rosehip and allowing the native forest to come back. The trees were kept low due to the harmful effect of local grazing cattle. Slowly and step by step, in our own woodshop, the big logs we bought from sustainable plantations were transformed into our houses, log cabins and furniture. A deep awe and respect for nature drove us to watch for every detail to protect her in all aspects we could, with the means we had at hand. There was so much to learn!! We made so many mistakes!! But we kept going on to fulfil the dream of doing, offering and opening to what we so much love: nature, beauty, the outdoors and activities, animals, a cosy and comfortable place to live, good and healthy food, harmony and to be close to like-minded people. Every step we took surprised us with unexpected hidden beauty. It was amazing to 'rediscover' what was already there but unseen in the thickness of the overgrown brush. And we tried to match this beauty with our best effort in what we built.

All I had done as an adult had to do with some kind of service and generating experiences; thus my inability to think in terms of business. My ex-husband was the one who handled that aspect and the early investment plan.

The big challenge came when, three years into the project, we divorced and I took full care of Peuma Hue together with my team, including its business side. Peuma Hue is far beyond a business to me and I don't think I ever learned much of that aspect; my mind still keeps thinking in terms of life experiences first. The economic side—it has to be economically self-sustainable, otherwise we cannot go on—has always been the hardest aspect for me. But being at Peuma Hue is a choice of life, and I'm grateful every day I open my eyes to be able to see what I can see from my window, come down the stairs to pat my dogs and cat, watch the smiles of everyone around. There are so many blessings and privileges in this enterprise that they counterbalance by far the hardship and extremely hard work it also involves. It hasn't been a blessing only for me. Most of the people working and visiting feel deeply affected and passionate about the place. So after everyone foretold I would be broke soon (my own fear as well), somehow we still manage to keep going! I can't take credit for it; there was no shortage of help of all sorts: ideas, suggestions, challenges and learning. As a team we kept on going; our guests, press, loyal travel agents and word of mouth kept referring our guests that help to keep this place alive.

Fourteen years later, Peuma Hue definitely encompasses all I and so many others value. Sharing it with my children and grandchildren is my best blessing, watching them run in freedom, playing with our dogs, kittens and horses, learning to appreciate the beauty of nature all around. The deep connection to nature—a mixture of peacefulness and grandeur—that people feel when stepping on its grounds; the loving connection our animals trigger even in those who used to be afraid of them; the closeness and friendship fostered among our guests and with our staff; the openness, relaxation and even transformation it awakens in everyone; the harmony between humans, animals and nature. So many guests and visitors refer to this place as 'being in another world'. And so do I.

The essence

My ex-husband is a lawyer and architecture is his hobby; I am a psychotherapist, life coach and former nature travel agent; in love with nature and the outdoors as much as what happens within ourselves. Both untiring travellers, we had been around the world visiting different places. We started the project already knowing it would be opened to tourists—to share it with the world and to be able to economically maintain it—but it would mainly be our home; opened to family, friends and those who appreciate majestic nature in the midst of one of the most stunning National Parks in the world.

So we began by renovating an old, derelict shack which became our temporary home, built our wood shop which transformed logs into our now 12 buildings (5 for guests), their furniture and everything we needed. It wasn't easy; it wasn't too well planned either. Tons of hard work and lots of personal commitment in the team we hired made it possible. But together with the son of a friend of mine who was like a foster son to me and who became our general manager for 12 years— an agriculture engineer and a climber himself—we took it on. We did the basic planning of the houses ourselves, taking into account the 360° views. So no matter where you are in the houses, you are always exposed to imposing natural sights. We found an architect that could interpret exactly what we had planned and improved on it, respected the style we wanted; blending logs, wood, stone and massive windows into just beautifully designed houses.

The project kept evolving; looking back it so much exceeds my wildest dreams in so many senses, good and challenging! Neither of us having formal training in either tourism or architecture, this enabled us to focus just on our hearts and on what we liked. Peuma Hue is the expression and the result of everything we care for and value. It is not a one-person enterprise. Every single person hired, working and visiting added and adds to what it has become and is still becoming; drawn by like-minded values of sustainability, concern for nature and a balanced way of life. I feel this place is not only my home; it is where I belong, it is my teacher, it is what structures me. And this happens not only to me, but also to so many of the people visiting, working or joining the team. I can even say that Peuma Hue shapes us as much as we shape Peuma, in a process of constant transformation, on both sides.

So what is Peuma Hue? It is an Eco-Lodge in a valley surrounded by mountains, pristine forest and waterfalls and with 2 miles of lakeshore; but it's also a place where people instantly relax, connect in different levels to themselves, to nature, to animals, to other guests, to staff, to everything around. It is a luxury ecolodge with healthy and balanced gourmet meals based on our organic garden and home-made products. It is a multi-activity destination where you can horseback ride with a horse whisperer; are led by golden retrievers on hikes that delight all guests; kayak in such a clear lake that you can see the bottom, with its sunken forest and trout swimming around; hike through 500 acres of pristine mountain forest trails with views over lakes, more mountains and valleys and that link with the largest hiking network in the country. It is a place where you can practise yoga under the steepest vertical drop of the area with rock needles jutting above or at an intimate Temple to Nature. It is a place where you make friends with people as much as with animals. Our guest book is full of references to how much the connection to our animals, to our staff and to other guests enhanced their experience, through interesting conversations at cocktails while everyone shares their day or life stories in a cosy living room that resembles a home and not a hotel. And yet there is more to it—quite intangible—that has to do with warmth, sharing, thoughtfulness, beauty, peacefulness, joy and also with what is beyond and exceeds us all. As a guest and travel agent put it in our guest book: 'please keep this place "hard to define"'; and another one, 'not mentioning God or Spirit once, this is the most spiritual place I've ever been'. For each person it is different and this is something we respect the most. We try to tap into what each one needs. What is important to us is that our guests have a meaningful time while here—within their own lifestyle and stage in their lives—and to be able to make at least a little difference.

But this was not that clear from the very beginning. Somehow it was in our hearts and values, but not laid down in a plan. Neither did we follow somebody else's predetermined model nor were we inspired to copy any given place. We started from scratch not only the real thing but the vision of it as well. Embedded in a spirit of connection and blending with nature, we tried to open what we loved to all those that could appreciate it and we tried to open ourselves to what was developing around. Peuma Hue means 'Place of Dreams' in native Mapuche language. But a 'peuma' is not any kind of dream; it is a dream that brings a message, conveys an answer to a quest; so it is a dream in the sense of *vision*. And this developed and keeps developing in all levels. Every place we cleared from the invasive rosehip surprised us with unbelievable beauty. Every house we built became a cosy home that everybody liked. Every activity or service we offer brings joy to the day. And the food we serve with our excellent regional wines triggers a compliment to our three chefs and to those who serve them with a smile. People come for a day and feel significantly touched. A volunteer who worked for three months wrote in our guest book 'This place changed my life'. It sounds unreal . . . It is not, but as everything on Earth, it always has two sides. It took us all these years to achieve not only a 'dream place' but a 'dream team'. During the journey, all sorts of things happened, hardships, mistakes, bad choices, people more suited for other paths, challenges of all sorts, unbalance . . . and some achievements as well!

How we started

The first three years were focused on clearing some of the land from introduced species, allowing the native forest to come back, fencing the land to keep cattle and poachers out, bringing in the infrastructure (there was no power nor energy source, no communication system), building the road (there was barely a 3 km trail from the main paved road to our entrance gate) and starting with our buildings and our organic vegetable garden. Following our own concern in preserving the land and waters and following all the National Park regulations, step by step and doing most of the work on site, it started to take shape. It took us about a year to build a big and a small house, plus all the clearing of rosehip around it.

We started by recycling a little shack that became our home for three years, building our woodshop and two staff houses. The rest followed, which today comprises two houses with four individual guest rooms each and three villas or elegant log cabins, totalling 14 rooms open to guests; our main dining and multi-purpose board room, main kitchen, laundry and pantry; our woodshop and workshop; five houses for staff including my own; a non-denominational temple; our stables and our boathouse. We couldn't afford all we wanted to equip it all, so we had to find our way of recycling old beautiful stuff found at warehouses or auctions, and buying things we liked from different cultures during our trips. The rest was built at home, at our woodshop. This resulted in quite an interesting blend of a rustic wood and stone architectural style with antiques and fine details opening through large windows to nature all around—quite different from what it would have been if decorated by a specialist—providing that homely feeling so treasured by our guests. Each room and house is different. When we bought or collected stuff, we had no plan where they would end. We bought or collected just what we liked. We also were grateful to receive beautiful objects from our relatives that had passed away: exquisite silver and china we share with our guests— much to my mother's dismay. So each time we finished a house, we just started placing things we had here and there, that just fitted perfectly; most of the rest, we designed ourselves and built at our woodshop or bought in the end. We started receiving guests slowly and progressively. At first it was friends, then friends of friends and word of mouth became—and still is—our best source of referrals.

Three years into the project, my husband and I divorced. What a huge challenge for me! How would I manage to carry on! I had no sense for business or investments, it was a huge enterprise and it scared me much. But facing fear has always been what allowed me to step towards a new stage in my life; so after quite a hard time, I kept on . . . again with tons of help from all around: my children, my extended family, my friends, my staff, even my ex-husband. Once we had the basic infrastructure—which kept and keeps changing every year with whatever we can afford and adding a little difference to the place—starting the business was the next step. Neither the manager at that time nor I had any idea of either marketing or how to do it. He focused basically on building, maintenance, gardening and administration; I focused on starting the tourist side: decoration, housekeeping, marketing, sales, activities, services and hosting.

Again, I followed my instincts and word of mouth was the huge support. People seemed to value what we offered and spread the word. The first five years, even though slowly, we kept growing. One of the huge challenges was to find the right staff, the core of the business. I am not easy, my standards are high and I wanted to offer the best at every level, with the best heart, the best attitude, the best team. At Peuma Hue, we are all animal people, so we kept having more animals (dogs, horses and cats) that started to become almost the most important part of our staff. All roaming free and extremely friendly with guests and with each other, they delight our guests and staff. Our horse whisperer trained the horses to be ridden, to swim with guests, to trust and be trusted—three so far were born here. My dogs, who always come with me on hikes, became the official 'hiking guides' and the most caring beings (four were born here, two on my couch). Our staff's dogs each 'work' in different fields: guiding and working with the horses, helping our gardener in the fields and learning to get along with each other. The cats and kittens are the main attraction for the younger ones. They too had to learn to get along with everybody else. Two sheep that think themselves horses— we all have some identity problems—joined our horse herd. Opening the impenetrable brush allowed more wildlife and birdlife to arrive on our grounds which became tamer and tamer, joining our friendly animal welcome.

I also wanted to have a positive impact in the community. Achieving the team we have today was not easy. Lots of good people came through Peuma Hue and with their efforts added to what it is today. We hired local people and tried to help our neighbours. A native community not far from us and descendants of native Mapuches had their homes in the area. A few more families joined the area. We met with them all, trying to foster a good relationship, which has deepened over time, helping each other in different ways. We founded, joined and fostered several local associations in town: we founded the first Tourist Consortium called 'South of the Nahuel Huapi' focused on sustainable tourism; we became members of an association of socially responsible businesses; and co-founded the Active Tourism Association and the Bureau for Corporate Active Tourism.

We try to encourage sustainable paradigms wherever we participate. We support a local foundation dedicated to the education of rural families, blending Mapuche and Western cultures together with practical tools that allow their graduates to go back to their families and communities improving their general welfare or moving on to different aspirations. We were then contacted by an international association that gathers volunteers from all over the world, studying and interested in working for sustainable and organic farms and eco-lodges. During the recent years of crisis after crisis, they have been another of our numerous blessings, not only helping to keep this place alive but enhancing and enriching what we are with their help and knowledge; and adding to the exchange of different cultures that meet at Peuma Hue—we receive guests from all over the world.

Peuma Hue throughout the years

Years followed with more and more time-consuming work and after 2008, we had several crises of all sorts one after the other—environmental, economic and political. Two volcanic eruptions in the area (one closing the airport for two months, the other for eight!!), international and national economic crises (85% of our guests are foreigners, mainly from the US and UK), avian flu and more, dropped our occupation rate to scary numbers. Our manager, after 12 years of hard work, was tired and quit; my dream team seemed not to materialise; I was quite worn out as well. My son stepped in, giving me the hugest and most loving support. Having his own successful and time-consuming socially responsible business himself, he always found time to help me, even though he lived across the globe. Having a much better sense for business and a very clear mind he helped—and is still helping—by supervising, suggesting and stepping in whenever I need it and when I have no clue. My two daughters also helped and supported in different ways. So did my son-in-law, friends and extended family. My grandchildren gave and give me joy. As I said before, I never lacked help. My own self-demanding 'type A' personality and high level of anxiety didn't make it easy to endure. Nature is where I recharge, where I get my insights, where I feel at my best. Our guests and loyal agents supported us by recommending us more and more and we barely made—and still make—it through. I met a wonderful man three years ago who has been the best companion and slowly we are still able to manage, even in the face of lots of challenges from outside—and sometimes from the inside as well.

Last year we finally managed to get our 'dream team' that matches our 'dream place'. I cannot be more grateful to our staff and family. They are the best, each one in its own field!

We do provide the best possible context for our guests and staff to have meaningful and wonderful experiences. We are internationally renowned in our field for providing very different life events; we have appeared in lots of international and national press; people feel instantly relaxed and at home as soon as they arrive. We have won many awards and have been featured in the press over the years. Among the awards we were chosen as one of the best 30 Eco-Lodges in the world; as the best sustainable luxury tourism company; in Trip Advisor we are among the first in popularity among all their hotels in Bariloche and in the last two years we won their Travelers' Choice award among the best small hotels in Argentina and South America; we were selected as one of the 14 best haciendas in South America, as one of the best 12 healthy retreats, as a green destination and as one of the 17 best hotels in Argentina. But we know there's still a lot to be done and not yet achieved in sustainable, social and economic matters. There's so much more I wish we could do!

We are still in a way, in 'surviving mode'. After eight months of airport closure following the volcanic eruption in Chile, the whole region was economically devastated. Economic difficulties in our area and in our country don't help a business like ours either. Even though we worked well and our occupancy rate rose dramatically after the airport reopened, we still barely close our numbers. Our maintenance costs rose by 100%, local exchange policies make it very hard to match our needs while keeping our rates as affordable as we can to encourage people to come. We have a limited number of accommodations to keep it so personalised and homely, which is what I like and what makes it so different. The place itself and all we offer has a high maintenance cost. To be able to render a high-quality service with the lowest possible number of staff we can afford does not allow time to participate more in community action as we used to in the beginning. Many other plans are set aside to cover the priorities.

From the beginning, my idea was to work with renewable and clean energy. Technical reasons and lack of means made it impossible when we started, having to bring the power line in from the main road and relying mainly on propane tanks, eight times the price of natural gas. Many mistakes made when we built the houses made them inefficient energy wise. Maintaining the huge property and all the houses, all the hiking and riding trails we opened, the entrance and inner roads, the organic vegetable garden and greenhouse, the lawn, harvesting, our vehicles and boats, salaries, taxes and all the services we provide, raise the costs to extremely high levels for what we can afford. So our next plan—and challenge—is to be more profitable without losing the spirit Peuma Hue has and that makes it so special.

Future plans

With our current team and with the reopening of our airport, we hope to be able to do better again, even in the face of hard economic times in our history and in our country. My own plan—we are not getting any younger—is to maintain the spirit of the place but delegate operations. I love my close contact with guests and staff, animals and nature. I want to develop more workshops in fields we like. We launched new yoga and nature retreats throughout the year, and are working on literary, photography and cooking workshops.

I also want to devote time to find a way to turn to renewable energy for ourselves and the community around. This needs time to gather the community, come up with a joint plan, develop a project, collect an initial investment and present it to our government to see if we can get some public support. I have had some advanced conversations at that level so I hope to be able to go forward with the project, which will be not only environmentally beneficial, but will help us economically and all the community around. We have a very nice relationship with all the community in our region, so that will help us to reach consensus.

Another plan is to add one more house to host more guests and my increasingly growing family, with my six grandchildren, when they visit. We want this house to be a model for sustainability and energy efficiency. Not having the means yet, it is still just a plan for the future. We also want to extend and develop further our organic garden and orchard to make it profitable in its own right. We wish to start selling our own home-made products such as jam and liqueurs. And who knows what will be coming up! It's already so much more than I ever dreamed of, that I'm sure it will keep expanding with the joint effort of all of us, trying always to impact as positively as we can in ourselves and around.

As for myself, I wish to take some more time for my partner, family, friends and myself; to travel again and attain more balance in my life as much as I want it for everybody else's. For all these years, Peuma Hue has taken up almost all of my time, more than is healthy. Many have suggested I write a book on the story of this place—which does trigger my enthusiasm . . . who knows if it will ever materialise, maybe this chapter might be a start.

I would like to be more involved in community and public matters eventually. So we have lots of further plans and dreams. I see Peuma Hue as a place that tries to provide the best possible context and the best possible quality at all levels, to make a little difference in people's lives (family, friends, staff, guests and community); our body, mind, emotions, spirit; nature, animals, activities and services; fostering well-being at every level and every being. As I said before, it works both ways: Peuma Hue keeps changing with everybody's input and it keeps changing us as well.

About the editors

Miguel Angel Gardetti PhD

 Miguel has been the head of the Center for Study of Corporate Sustainability (IESC) since its foundation in 2002, and he also holds the same position at the Center for Study of Sustainable Luxury. He is head professor in MBA and masters' programmes both in Argentina and abroad. He has provided training within frameworks of executive education and in house programmes to CEOs and corporate managers from both domestic and multinational companies in Argentina and Latin America.

In the field of luxury and sustainability, he has lectured at the Instituto de Empresa (Madrid, Spain), one of the top business schools in Europe. He was also a speaker at Identidad Uruguay, an event organised by the Universidad de Empresa (Montevideo), with a lecture on fashion, luxury and sustainability. He was the creator of the Best Performance in Sustainable Luxury in Latin America Award (at present evolving towards the Award in Sustainable Premium and Luxury at a global level). He has also developed several publications in the area of sustainable luxury.

Miguel was a member of the United Nations Global Compact Promoting Group in Argentina and a member of its governance body—the Board of the Argentine Chapter of The Global Compact—for two consecutive terms. He was co-founder of the Global Compact Chair in Argentina, and he was also part of the task force that developed the 'Management Responsible Education Principles' of the United Nations Global Compact.

He has also coordinated tasks for the Inter-American Development Bank, the International Finance Corporation (private sector arm of the World Bank), the Netherlands Development Organisation, the United Nations (New York), and the World Resources Institute (USA).

María Eugenia Girón

María Eugenia Girón is Executive Director of the Instituto de Empresa (IE) Business School Premium and Prestige Business Centre, sponsored by MasterCard. She also teaches 'Premium, Luxury and Creative Venture Entrepreneurship' at IE Business School and has been a member of the Board of Trustees of IE University since 2009.

Ms Girón has over 18 years' experience in premium and luxury goods companies. She has led and operated successfully as a CEO business and brand turnaround expert and has advised numerous luxury companies on strategic development, global brand building and expansion into Asia.

She led the acquisition of Le Chameau and subsequently served as Executive Chairman of this leading French brand of premium rubber boots and rainwear. Le Chameau was the first investment of the Silvercloud fund for which she was an advisor.

Ms Girón led the management buy-in of Carrera y Carrera in 1999 with private equity group 3i. She turned the company into a global luxury brand. Her previous experience in the luxury goods industry was at Loewe, the leading Spanish company. While attending Harvard Business School, she was a consultant with the Guggenheim Museum and the Estée Lauder Company.

She is committed to entrepreneurship and is involved in several early-stage investments. In 2013, she was a member of the investors' panel on the Spanish *Dragons' Den* television series, which featured entrepreneurs pitching business ideas to secure finance from a panel of investors.

She is a member of the International Board of OCEANA, a leading environmental organisation and member of YPO/WPO. She is also a Board member of Fundación para la Diversidad, the Spain Start-Up Summit, an Advisor to Ashoka, and former Advisory Board member of the Stowe School's Madrid Campus.

Ms Girón is the author of *Secretos de Lujo (Inside Luxury*; 2009), and director and co-author of the *Diccionario del Lujo y Responsabilidad (Dictionary for Luxury and Responsibility*; 2012). She writes a biweekly blog for the magazine *Forbes México* and is an active lecturer, teacher and advisor at various universities and business schools. She was awarded Best Woman Executive of Spain in 2004.

She received both an undergraduate and master's degree in Engineering from ICAI Universidad Pontificia de Comillas and a MBA degree from Harvard Business School.

Ms Girón and her husband have three children and live in Madrid.